50 Vegan Holiday Recipes for Home

By: Kelly Johnson

Table of Contents

- Vegan Wellington
- Stuffed Butternut Squash
- Mushroom Gravy
- Roasted Vegetable Salad
- Vegan Cheese Platter
- Cranberry Orange Sauce
- Lentil Loaf
- Pumpkin Soup
- Vegan Stuffing
- Sweet Potato Casserole
- Green Bean Almondine
- Quinoa Salad
- Maple Glazed Carrots
- Vegan Shepherd's Pie
- Cauliflower Mashed Potatoes
- Garlic Rosemary Roasted Potatoes
- Baked Apples with Cinnamon
- Vegan Pecan Pie
- Chocolate Avocado Mousse
- Holiday Fruit Salad
- Vegan Eggnog
- Gingerbread Cookies
- Mulled Wine
- Roasted Brussels Sprouts with Balsamic Glaze
- Vegan Tiramisu
- Pomegranate Salad
- Stuffed Portobello Mushrooms
- Vegan Truffles
- Roasted Chestnuts
- Spinach Artichoke Dip
- Herb Roasted Acorn Squash
- Vegan Gravy
- Pear and Arugula Salad
- Glazed Tofu Ham
- Vegan Mac and Cheese

- Peppermint Chocolate Bark
- Cinnamon Rolls
- Vegan Pumpkin Pie
- Roasted Beet Salad
- Coconut Whipped Cream
- Stuffed Bell Peppers
- Vegan Yorkshire Pudding
- Holiday Spice Cake
- Quinoa Stuffed Acorn Squash
- Vegan Gingersnaps
- Cranberry Walnut Bread
- Vegan Biscuits with Mushroom Gravy
- Chocolate Peppermint Cupcakes
- Apple Cranberry Crisp
- Spiced Hot Chocolate

Vegan Wellington

Ingredients:

- **For the Wellington:**
    - 1 sheet vegan puff pastry, thawed if frozen
    - 1 cup cooked lentils (green or brown), drained
    - 1 cup mushrooms, finely chopped (such as cremini or portobello)
    - 1 onion, finely chopped
    - 2 cloves garlic, minced
    - 1 tablespoon soy sauce or tamari
    - 1 tablespoon olive oil
    - 1 teaspoon dried thyme
    - Salt and pepper to taste
    - Flour for dusting
- **For the Mushroom Duxelles:**
    - 1 cup mushrooms, finely chopped
    - 1 shallot, finely chopped
    - 1 clove garlic, minced
    - 1 tablespoon olive oil
    - Salt and pepper to taste
- **For Assembly:**
    - Dijon mustard
    - Vegan puff pastry, rolled out into a rectangle (large enough to wrap around the filling)
    - Vegan egg wash (optional; can use almond milk or soy milk for brushing)

Instructions:

1. **Prepare the Filling:**
    - Heat olive oil in a pan over medium heat. Add chopped onions and cook until translucent, about 5 minutes.
    - Add minced garlic and cook for another 1-2 minutes until fragrant.
    - Add chopped mushrooms, soy sauce, dried thyme, salt, and pepper. Cook until mushrooms are tender and most of the moisture has evaporated, about 8-10 minutes.
    - Stir in cooked lentils and cook for another 2-3 minutes until well combined. Remove from heat and let cool.
2. **Make the Mushroom Duxelles:**

- Heat olive oil in a separate pan over medium heat. Add shallots and cook until softened, about 3-4 minutes.
- Add minced garlic and cook for another 1-2 minutes.
- Add chopped mushrooms, salt, and pepper. Cook until mushrooms release their moisture and the mixture becomes thick, about 10-12 minutes. Stir frequently to prevent sticking. Remove from heat and let cool.

3. **Assemble the Wellington:**
    - Preheat your oven to 400°F (200°C).
    - Roll out the puff pastry sheet on a lightly floured surface into a rectangle large enough to wrap around the filling.
    - Spread a thin layer of Dijon mustard over the pastry sheet.
    - Spread the cooled lentil-mushroom mixture evenly over the pastry, leaving about 1 inch of space around the edges.
    - Top the lentil mixture with the cooled mushroom duxelles, spreading evenly.

4. **Wrap and Bake:**
    - Carefully roll the puff pastry over the filling, starting from one long side, until you have a sealed log shape. Press the edges to seal.
    - Place the Wellington seam side down on a baking sheet lined with parchment paper.
    - Optional: Brush the top of the Wellington with vegan egg wash (almond milk or soy milk).
    - Bake in the preheated oven for 30-35 minutes, or until the pastry is golden brown and crispy.
    - Remove from the oven and let it rest for a few minutes before slicing.

5. **Serve:**
    - Slice the Vegan Wellington into thick slices and serve with your favorite vegan gravy or sauce.

Enjoy your Vegan Wellington as a centerpiece for a special holiday meal!

Stuffed Butternut Squash

Ingredients:

- 2 medium-sized butternut squashes
- 1 cup quinoa, rinsed
- 2 cups vegetable broth or water
- 1 tablespoon olive oil
- 1 onion, diced
- 2 cloves garlic, minced
- 1 red bell pepper, diced
- 1 zucchini, diced
- 1 cup mushrooms, chopped
- 1 teaspoon dried thyme
- 1 teaspoon dried sage
- Salt and pepper, to taste
- 1/2 cup chopped fresh parsley
- 1/2 cup chopped walnuts or pecans (optional)
- 1/4 cup dried cranberries or raisins (optional)
- Vegan cheese (optional, for topping)

Instructions:

1. **Prepare the Squash:**
    - Preheat your oven to 400°F (200°C).
    - Cut the butternut squash in half lengthwise and scoop out the seeds and fibers. Place the squash halves cut-side down on a baking sheet lined with parchment paper. Bake for 30-40 minutes, or until the squash is tender when pierced with a fork. Remove from the oven and let cool slightly.
2. **Prepare the Quinoa:**
    - While the squash is baking, rinse the quinoa under cold water using a fine mesh sieve.
    - In a medium saucepan, bring the vegetable broth or water to a boil. Add the rinsed quinoa, reduce heat to low, cover, and simmer for 15-20 minutes, or until the quinoa is cooked and the liquid is absorbed. Remove from heat and fluff with a fork.
3. **Make the Stuffing:**
    - Heat olive oil in a large skillet over medium heat. Add diced onion and cook until translucent, about 5 minutes.

- Add minced garlic and cook for another 1-2 minutes until fragrant.
- Add diced bell pepper, zucchini, and mushrooms to the skillet. Cook for 5-7 minutes, stirring occasionally, until the vegetables are tender.
- Stir in dried thyme, dried sage, salt, and pepper to taste. Cook for another minute to let the flavors meld together.
- Remove the skillet from heat and stir in the cooked quinoa, chopped parsley, chopped nuts (if using), and dried cranberries or raisins (if using). Adjust seasoning if needed.

4. **Assemble and Bake:**
   - Flip the baked butternut squash halves over so they are cut-side up on the baking sheet.
   - Fill each squash half generously with the quinoa and vegetable stuffing mixture.
   - If desired, sprinkle vegan cheese on top of each stuffed squash half.

5. **Final Bake:**
   - Return the stuffed squash halves to the oven and bake for an additional 10-15 minutes, or until heated through and the cheese (if using) is melted and bubbly.

6. **Serve:**
   - Remove from the oven and let cool for a few minutes before serving. Garnish with additional chopped parsley or nuts if desired.

This stuffed butternut squash dish is not only visually appealing but also packed with flavors and textures that will impress your guests during the holidays!

Mushroom Gravy

Ingredients:

- 2 cups mushrooms, finely chopped (such as cremini or button mushrooms)
- 1 onion, finely chopped
- 2 cloves garlic, minced
- 2 tablespoons olive oil or vegan butter
- 2 tablespoons all-purpose flour (or gluten-free flour for GF option)
- 2 cups vegetable broth
- 1 tablespoon soy sauce or tamari
- 1 teaspoon dried thyme
- Salt and pepper, to taste
- Fresh parsley or thyme for garnish (optional)

Instructions:

1. **Sauté the Mushrooms and Onions:**
    - Heat olive oil or vegan butter in a large skillet over medium heat.
    - Add chopped onions and cook until translucent, about 5-7 minutes.
    - Add minced garlic and cook for another 1-2 minutes until fragrant.
    - Add chopped mushrooms to the skillet and cook for 5-7 minutes, stirring occasionally, until mushrooms release their moisture and become tender.
2. **Make the Gravy:**
    - Sprinkle the flour over the mushroom mixture in the skillet. Stir well to coat the mushrooms and cook for 1-2 minutes to lightly toast the flour.
    - Gradually pour in the vegetable broth, stirring constantly to avoid lumps.
    - Stir in soy sauce or tamari, dried thyme, salt, and pepper to taste.
    - Bring the gravy to a simmer. Cook for 5-7 minutes, stirring occasionally, until the gravy thickens to your desired consistency.
3. **Adjust Seasoning and Serve:**
    - Taste and adjust seasoning if needed, adding more salt, pepper, or thyme according to your preference.
    - Remove from heat and garnish with fresh parsley or thyme if desired.
4. **Serve Warm:**
    - Serve the mushroom gravy warm over mashed potatoes, roasted vegetables, vegan Wellington, or any other dish of your choice.

This vegan mushroom gravy is rich, savory, and packed with mushroom flavor, making it a perfect addition to your holiday table or any meal where you want to add a delicious gravy!

Roasted Vegetable Salad

Ingredients:

- **For the Salad:**
    - 1 small eggplant, diced
    - 1 zucchini, diced
    - 1 red bell pepper, diced
    - 1 yellow bell pepper, diced
    - 1 red onion, sliced
    - 1 cup cherry tomatoes, halved
    - 2 tablespoons olive oil
    - Salt and pepper, to taste
    - Mixed greens (such as spinach, arugula, or lettuce)
- **For the Dressing:**
    - 3 tablespoons balsamic vinegar
    - 2 tablespoons olive oil
    - 1 tablespoon Dijon mustard
    - 1 clove garlic, minced
    - Salt and pepper, to taste
- **Optional Toppings:**
    - Toasted pine nuts or walnuts
    - Fresh herbs (such as basil or parsley)
    - Vegan feta or dairy-free cheese (optional)

Instructions:

1. **Preheat the Oven:**
    - Preheat your oven to 400°F (200°C).
2. **Prepare the Vegetables:**
    - In a large mixing bowl, combine diced eggplant, zucchini, red bell pepper, yellow bell pepper, red onion, and cherry tomatoes.
    - Drizzle olive oil over the vegetables and toss to coat evenly. Season with salt and pepper to taste.
3. **Roast the Vegetables:**
    - Spread the vegetables in a single layer on a baking sheet lined with parchment paper.
    - Roast in the preheated oven for 20-25 minutes, or until the vegetables are tender and slightly caramelized, stirring halfway through.

4. **Make the Dressing:**
   - In a small bowl, whisk together balsamic vinegar, olive oil, Dijon mustard, minced garlic, salt, and pepper until well combined.
5. **Assemble the Salad:**
   - In a large salad bowl, arrange a bed of mixed greens.
   - Top the greens with the roasted vegetables.
6. **Finish and Serve:**
   - Drizzle the dressing over the salad just before serving.
   - Optional: Garnish with toasted pine nuts or walnuts, fresh herbs, and vegan feta or dairy-free cheese if desired.
7. **Enjoy:**
   - Toss gently to combine and serve the roasted vegetable salad immediately.

This roasted vegetable salad is not only vibrant and flavorful but also packed with nutrients and textures that make it a satisfying dish on its own or as a side for a holiday meal. Adjust the ingredients and toppings according to your taste preferences and enjoy!

Vegan Cheese Platter

Components for Vegan Cheese Platter:

1. **Variety of Vegan Cheeses:**
    - Choose a selection of vegan cheeses such as:
        - Cashew cheese (plain, herbed, or flavored)
        - Almond cheese
        - Coconut cheese
        - Nut-based cheese spreads
        - Vegan cream cheese (plain or flavored)
2. **Accompaniments:**
    - **Fresh Fruits:** Grapes, strawberries, apple slices, pear slices.
    - **Dried Fruits:** Fig slices, apricots, dates.
    - **Nuts:** Walnuts, almonds, cashews.
    - **Olives:** Kalamata olives, green olives, stuffed olives.
    - **Pickles:** Cornichons, pickled onions, pickled vegetables.
    - **Crackers:** Assorted varieties such as whole wheat, gluten-free, or seed crackers.
    - **Bread:** Slices of baguette or artisan bread, toasted if desired.
    - **Crispy snacks:** Rice crackers, vegetable chips.
3. **Garnishes:**
    - Fresh herbs (rosemary, thyme, basil) for decoration and flavor enhancement.
    - Edible flowers for a beautiful presentation.

Assembly Instructions:

1. **Prepare the Cheeses:**
    - Arrange the different types of vegan cheeses on a large platter or wooden board. You can slice some cheeses and leave others whole or in chunks for variety.
2. **Add Accompaniments:**
    - Surround the vegan cheeses with fresh fruits, dried fruits, nuts, olives, pickles, and crackers. Arrange them in a visually appealing manner around the cheeses.
3. **Garnish:**

- Sprinkle fresh herbs over the cheeses and around the platter for added freshness and aroma. Edible flowers can be used sparingly to add a pop of color.

4. **Serve:**
    - Place small cheese knives or spreaders near the cheeses for easy serving.
    - Optionally, provide a description of each cheese and its accompaniments for guests to enjoy.

Tips for a Great Vegan Cheese Platter:

- **Variety:** Aim for a variety of flavors, textures, and colors to make the platter visually appealing and enjoyable.
- **Balance:** Include a balance of sweet and savory elements to complement the cheeses.
- **Temperature:** Bring the cheeses to room temperature before serving to enhance their flavors and textures.
- **Customization:** Feel free to customize the platter based on seasonal fruits, personal preferences, and dietary restrictions.

By following these guidelines, you can create a stunning and delicious vegan cheese platter that will impress your guests and make for a delightful addition to any holiday celebration or gathering.

Cranberry Orange Sauce

Ingredients:

- 12 ounces (about 3 cups) fresh or frozen cranberries
- 1 cup orange juice (freshly squeezed is best)
- Zest of 1 orange
- 1/2 cup granulated sugar (adjust to taste)
- 1 cinnamon stick (optional)
- Pinch of salt

Instructions:

1. **Combine Ingredients:**
   - In a medium saucepan, combine the cranberries, orange juice, orange zest, sugar, cinnamon stick (if using), and a pinch of salt.
2. **Cook the Sauce:**
   - Bring the mixture to a boil over medium-high heat, stirring occasionally.
3. **Simmer:**
   - Reduce the heat to medium-low and let the sauce simmer for about 10-15 minutes, or until the cranberries burst and the sauce thickens to your desired consistency. Stir occasionally to prevent sticking.
4. **Adjust Sweetness:**
   - Taste the sauce and adjust sweetness if needed by adding more sugar, a tablespoon at a time, stirring well until dissolved.
5. **Cool and Serve:**
   - Remove the saucepan from heat and let the cranberry orange sauce cool to room temperature. It will continue to thicken as it cools.
6. **Serve:**
   - Transfer the cranberry orange sauce to a serving dish or jar. Remove the cinnamon stick if used before serving.
7. **Enjoy:**
   - Serve the cranberry orange sauce chilled or at room temperature alongside your favorite holiday dishes or desserts.

Tips:

- **Variations:** For a twist, you can add a splash of vanilla extract or a pinch of ground cloves or nutmeg.

- **Make Ahead:** Cranberry orange sauce can be made ahead of time and stored in the refrigerator for up to a week. Bring it to room temperature before serving.
- **Texture:** If you prefer a smoother sauce, you can blend it briefly with an immersion blender or in a regular blender after cooking.

This vegan cranberry orange sauce is a delightful addition to your holiday table, bringing a burst of tangy-sweet flavor that complements a variety of savory and sweet dishes.

Lentil Loaf

Ingredients:

- 1 cup dried green or brown lentils, rinsed
- 2 1/2 cups vegetable broth or water
- 1 tablespoon olive oil
- 1 onion, finely chopped
- 2-3 garlic cloves, minced
- 1 carrot, grated
- 1 celery stalk, finely chopped
- 1 bell pepper, finely chopped (any color)
- 1 cup rolled oats (gluten-free if needed)
- 1/2 cup breadcrumbs (gluten-free if needed)
- 1/4 cup ground flaxseed
- 1/4 cup nutritional yeast
- 2 tablespoons tomato paste or ketchup
- 1 tablespoon soy sauce or tamari
- 1 teaspoon dried thyme
- 1 teaspoon dried oregano
- 1/2 teaspoon smoked paprika
- Salt and pepper, to taste
- BBQ sauce or ketchup, for topping (optional)

Instructions:

1. **Cook the Lentils:**
   - In a medium saucepan, combine the lentils and vegetable broth or water. Bring to a boil over medium-high heat.
   - Reduce the heat to low, cover, and simmer for 25-30 minutes, or until the lentils are tender and the liquid is absorbed. Drain any excess liquid and let cool slightly.
2. **Prepare the Vegetables:**
   - Preheat your oven to 350°F (175°C).
   - Heat olive oil in a large skillet over medium heat. Add the chopped onion and cook until translucent, about 5-7 minutes.
   - Add minced garlic, grated carrot, chopped celery, and bell pepper to the skillet. Cook for another 5-7 minutes, or until the vegetables are softened. Remove from heat and let cool slightly.

3. **Mix the Loaf Mixture:**
   - In a large mixing bowl, combine the cooked lentils, sautéed vegetables, rolled oats, breadcrumbs, ground flaxseed, nutritional yeast, tomato paste or ketchup, soy sauce or tamari, dried thyme, dried oregano, smoked paprika, salt, and pepper.
   - Mix well until everything is evenly combined. Taste and adjust seasoning if needed.
4. **Form the Lentil Loaf:**
   - Lightly grease a loaf pan with olive oil or line it with parchment paper.
   - Transfer the lentil mixture into the loaf pan, pressing it down firmly and smoothing the top with a spoon or spatula.
   - Optional: Brush the top of the lentil loaf with BBQ sauce or ketchup for added flavor and a caramelized finish.
5. **Bake the Lentil Loaf:**
   - Bake in the preheated oven for 45-55 minutes, or until the lentil loaf is firm and the top is golden brown.
   - Remove from the oven and let it cool in the pan for 10-15 minutes before slicing.
6. **Serve:**
   - Carefully slice the lentil loaf and serve warm with your favorite sides, such as mashed potatoes, roasted vegetables, or salad.

This vegan lentil loaf is hearty, nutritious, and packed with flavor, making it a wonderful main dish for any holiday or gathering. Enjoy!

Pumpkin Soup

Ingredients:

- 1 tablespoon olive oil
- 1 onion, chopped
- 3 cloves garlic, minced
- 1 tablespoon fresh ginger, grated (optional)
- 4 cups (about 1 kg) pumpkin puree (canned or homemade)
- 3 cups vegetable broth
- 1 cup coconut milk (full-fat for creaminess)
- 1 tablespoon maple syrup or agave syrup (optional, for a touch of sweetness)
- 1 teaspoon ground cumin
- 1/2 teaspoon ground cinnamon
- 1/4 teaspoon ground nutmeg
- Salt and pepper, to taste
- Fresh herbs (such as parsley or cilantro), for garnish
- Coconut cream or vegan yogurt, for garnish (optional)

Instructions:

1. **Sauté Aromatics:**
   - Heat olive oil in a large pot over medium heat. Add chopped onion and sauté until translucent, about 5-7 minutes.
   - Add minced garlic and grated ginger (if using), and sauté for another 1-2 minutes until fragrant.
2. **Add Pumpkin and Spices:**
   - Stir in the pumpkin puree, ground cumin, ground cinnamon, and ground nutmeg. Cook for 2-3 minutes, stirring occasionally to combine the flavors.
3. **Simmer:**
   - Pour in the vegetable broth and bring the mixture to a simmer. Let it cook for 15-20 minutes, stirring occasionally, until the soup has slightly thickened and flavors have melded together.
4. **Blend the Soup:**
   - Remove the pot from heat. Using an immersion blender, blend the soup until smooth and creamy. Alternatively, carefully transfer the soup in batches to a blender and blend until smooth. Be cautious with hot liquids.
5. **Add Coconut Milk and Sweetener:**

- Return the blended soup to low heat. Stir in the coconut milk and maple syrup or agave syrup (if using). Allow the soup to heat through, but do not boil.

6. **Season and Serve:**
    - Season the pumpkin soup with salt and pepper to taste. Adjust the spices or sweetness if needed.
    - Ladle the soup into bowls. Garnish with fresh herbs and a swirl of coconut cream or vegan yogurt if desired.
7. **Enjoy:**
    - Serve the warm and creamy vegan pumpkin soup as a starter or main dish, accompanied by crusty bread or your favorite salad.

This vegan pumpkin soup is rich, velvety, and filled with warm spices, making it a comforting addition to any holiday meal or cozy evening at home.

Vegan Stuffing

Ingredients:

- 1 loaf of day-old bread (about 12-16 ounces), cubed (choose a vegan-friendly bread)
- 2 tablespoons olive oil or vegan butter
- 1 onion, diced
- 3-4 cloves garlic, minced
- 2 celery stalks, diced
- 1 carrot, diced
- 8 ounces mushrooms, chopped
- 1 tablespoon fresh sage, chopped (or 1 teaspoon dried sage)
- 1 tablespoon fresh thyme leaves (or 1 teaspoon dried thyme)
- 1 teaspoon dried rosemary
- Salt and pepper, to taste
- 1 1/2 - 2 cups vegetable broth
- Fresh parsley, chopped, for garnish

Instructions:

1. **Prepare the Bread:**
    - Preheat your oven to 350°F (175°C).
    - Spread the cubed bread on a baking sheet and bake for about 10-15 minutes, until slightly toasted. This step helps the bread absorb the flavors without getting soggy later.
2. **Sauté Vegetables:**
    - In a large skillet or frying pan, heat olive oil or vegan butter over medium heat.
    - Add diced onion and sauté for 5-7 minutes until translucent and fragrant.
    - Add minced garlic, diced celery, diced carrot, and chopped mushrooms to the skillet. Cook for another 5-7 minutes until the vegetables are tender.
3. **Seasoning:**
    - Stir in chopped sage, thyme leaves, dried rosemary, salt, and pepper. Cook for another 1-2 minutes until the herbs are fragrant.
4. **Combine:**
    - In a large mixing bowl, combine the toasted bread cubes with the sautéed vegetable mixture. Mix well to distribute the vegetables and herbs evenly.
5. **Moisten:**

- Gradually pour vegetable broth over the bread mixture, starting with 1 1/2 cups. Gently toss the mixture until the bread absorbs the broth and becomes moistened. Add more broth if needed, but be careful not to make it too soggy.

6. **Bake:**
   - Transfer the stuffing mixture into a greased baking dish. Cover with foil and bake in the preheated oven for 25-30 minutes.
7. **Finish and Serve:**
   - Remove the foil and bake for an additional 10-15 minutes, or until the top is golden brown and crispy.
   - Garnish with chopped fresh parsley before serving.
8. **Enjoy:**
   - Serve the vegan stuffing warm as a delicious side dish for your holiday meal.

This vegan stuffing is packed with savory flavors from the herbs and vegetables, making it a comforting and satisfying addition to any festive table. Adjust the seasonings and add your favorite nuts or dried fruits for additional texture and flavor if desired.

Sweet Potato Casserole

Ingredients:

- **For the Sweet Potato Base:**
    - 3-4 large sweet potatoes, peeled and diced
    - 1/4 cup coconut milk (canned, full-fat)
    - 1/4 cup maple syrup or agave syrup
    - 1 teaspoon vanilla extract
    - 1/2 teaspoon ground cinnamon
    - 1/4 teaspoon ground nutmeg
    - Salt, to taste
- **For the Topping:**
    - 1 cup pecans or walnuts, chopped
    - 1/2 cup old-fashioned oats (gluten-free if needed)
    - 1/4 cup brown sugar or coconut sugar
    - 2 tablespoons vegan butter or coconut oil, melted
    - 1/2 teaspoon ground cinnamon
    - Pinch of salt

Instructions:

1. **Prepare the Sweet Potatoes:**
    - Preheat your oven to 375°F (190°C).
    - Place the diced sweet potatoes in a large pot and cover with water. Bring to a boil over high heat, then reduce the heat to medium-low and simmer for 15-20 minutes, or until the sweet potatoes are tender when pierced with a fork.
    - Drain the sweet potatoes and transfer them to a large mixing bowl.
2. **Mash and Season:**
    - Mash the sweet potatoes using a potato masher or fork until smooth.
    - Stir in coconut milk, maple syrup or agave syrup, vanilla extract, ground cinnamon, ground nutmeg, and salt to taste. Mix well until everything is thoroughly combined.
3. **Prepare the Topping:**
    - In a separate bowl, combine chopped pecans or walnuts, oats, brown sugar or coconut sugar, melted vegan butter or coconut oil, ground cinnamon, and a pinch of salt. Mix until the topping mixture is crumbly and well combined.

4. **Assemble and Bake:**
    - Transfer the mashed sweet potato mixture to a greased baking dish, spreading it out evenly.
    - Sprinkle the topping mixture evenly over the sweet potatoes.
5. **Bake:**
    - Bake in the preheated oven for 25-30 minutes, or until the topping is golden brown and crispy.
6. **Serve:**
    - Remove from the oven and let it cool for a few minutes before serving.
    - Serve the sweet potato casserole warm as a delicious side dish or dessert.

This vegan sweet potato casserole is rich, creamy, and topped with a crunchy, sweet-nutty topping that adds wonderful texture and flavor. It's sure to be a hit at your next holiday gathering!

Green Bean Almondine

Ingredients:

- 1 lb (about 450g) fresh green beans, ends trimmed
- 1/2 cup sliced almonds
- 2 tablespoons olive oil
- 2 tablespoons vegan butter
- 2 garlic cloves, minced
- Zest of 1 lemon
- 1 tablespoon lemon juice
- Salt and pepper, to taste
- Fresh parsley, chopped, for garnish (optional)

Instructions:

1. **Blanch the Green Beans:**
    - Bring a large pot of salted water to a boil. Add the trimmed green beans and cook for about 3-4 minutes, until they are bright green and crisp-tender. Immediately transfer the green beans to a bowl of ice water to stop the cooking process. Drain and set aside.
2. **Toast the Almonds:**
    - In a large skillet, dry-toast the sliced almonds over medium heat for 2-3 minutes, stirring frequently, until they are lightly golden and fragrant. Transfer the toasted almonds to a plate and set aside.
3. **Sauté the Green Beans:**
    - In the same skillet, heat olive oil and vegan butter over medium heat until the butter is melted.
    - Add minced garlic to the skillet and sauté for about 1 minute, until fragrant.
4. **Combine and Season:**
    - Add the blanched green beans to the skillet. Toss to coat them evenly with the garlic-infused oil and butter.
    - Stir in lemon zest and lemon juice. Season with salt and pepper to taste.
5. **Serve:**
    - Transfer the green beans almondine to a serving dish. Sprinkle the toasted almonds over the top.
    - Garnish with chopped fresh parsley if desired.
6. **Enjoy:**

- Serve the green bean almondine warm as a delightful side dish alongside your favorite main course.

This vegan green bean almondine is flavorful, vibrant, and showcases the natural sweetness of green beans paired with crunchy almonds and zesty lemon. It's perfect for any holiday or special occasion meal!

Quinoa Salad

Ingredients:

- 1 cup quinoa, rinsed
- 2 cups water or vegetable broth
- 1 can (15 ounces) chickpeas, drained and rinsed
- 1 cup cherry tomatoes, halved
- 1 cucumber, diced
- 1/2 red onion, finely chopped
- 1/2 cup fresh parsley, chopped
- 1/4 cup fresh mint leaves, chopped (optional)
- 1/4 cup kalamata olives, sliced (optional)
- 1/4 cup roasted almonds or pine nuts, chopped (optional)

For the Dressing:

- 1/4 cup extra virgin olive oil
- 2 tablespoons lemon juice (about 1 lemon)
- 1 clove garlic, minced
- 1 teaspoon Dijon mustard
- 1 teaspoon maple syrup or agave syrup (optional, for sweetness)
- Salt and pepper, to taste

Instructions:

1. **Cook the Quinoa:**
    - In a medium saucepan, combine the quinoa and water or vegetable broth. Bring to a boil over medium-high heat.
    - Reduce the heat to low, cover, and simmer for 15-20 minutes, or until the quinoa is cooked and the liquid is absorbed. Remove from heat and let it cool.
2. **Prepare the Salad Ingredients:**
    - In a large mixing bowl, combine the cooked quinoa, chickpeas, cherry tomatoes, cucumber, red onion, parsley, mint leaves (if using), kalamata olives (if using), and roasted almonds or pine nuts (if using). Toss gently to mix.
3. **Make the Dressing:**

- In a small bowl or jar, whisk together the olive oil, lemon juice, minced garlic, Dijon mustard, maple syrup or agave syrup (if using), salt, and pepper until well combined.
4. **Combine and Chill:**
    - Pour the dressing over the quinoa salad mixture. Toss gently until everything is evenly coated with the dressing.
5. **Chill and Serve:**
    - Cover the quinoa salad and refrigerate for at least 30 minutes to allow the flavors to meld together.
    - Before serving, taste and adjust seasoning if needed. You can garnish with additional fresh herbs or nuts if desired.
6. **Enjoy:**
    - Serve the quinoa salad chilled or at room temperature as a nutritious and delicious side dish or main course.

This vegan quinoa salad is packed with protein, fiber, and fresh flavors, making it a perfect addition to any meal or as a standalone dish for lunch or dinner. It's versatile and can be customized with your favorite vegetables and toppings.

Maple Glazed Carrots

Ingredients:

- 1 lb (about 450g) carrots, peeled and sliced into rounds or sticks
- 2 tablespoons vegan butter or olive oil
- 3 tablespoons maple syrup
- 1 tablespoon balsamic vinegar (optional, for a touch of acidity)
- Salt and pepper, to taste
- Fresh parsley or thyme, chopped, for garnish (optional)

Instructions:

1. **Prepare the Carrots:**
    - Peel the carrots and slice them into rounds or sticks, whichever you prefer. Try to make them of uniform thickness for even cooking.
2. **Cook the Carrots:**
    - In a large skillet or frying pan, melt the vegan butter or heat the olive oil over medium heat.
    - Add the sliced carrots to the skillet and sauté for 3-4 minutes, stirring occasionally, until they start to soften slightly.
3. **Add Maple Syrup:**
    - Drizzle the maple syrup over the carrots in the skillet. If using balsamic vinegar, add it now as well.
    - Stir to coat the carrots evenly with the maple syrup mixture.
4. **Simmer and Glaze:**
    - Reduce the heat to medium-low and let the carrots simmer gently in the maple syrup mixture for 8-10 minutes, or until the carrots are tender and the maple syrup has thickened into a glaze, stirring occasionally.
5. **Season and Serve:**
    - Season the maple glazed carrots with salt and pepper to taste.
    - Garnish with chopped fresh parsley or thyme if desired.
6. **Enjoy:**
    - Serve the maple glazed carrots warm as a delicious side dish alongside your favorite main course.

Tips:

- **Variations:** You can add a pinch of ground cinnamon or ground ginger for extra flavor.

- **Texture:** Adjust the cooking time to achieve your preferred level of tenderness for the carrots.
- **Presentation:** Garnish with additional herbs or a sprinkle of toasted nuts for added texture and flavor.

This vegan maple glazed carrots recipe is simple to make and adds a touch of sweetness and elegance to any meal. It's perfect for holiday dinners or anytime you want to enjoy a comforting and flavorful vegetable dish.

Vegan Shepherd's Pie

Ingredients:

For the Mashed Potatoes:

- 2 lbs (about 1 kg) potatoes, peeled and chopped into chunks
- 1/2 cup unsweetened almond milk or other non-dairy milk
- 2 tablespoons vegan butter
- Salt and pepper, to taste

For the Filling:

- 1 tablespoon olive oil
- 1 onion, chopped
- 3 cloves garlic, minced
- 2 carrots, diced
- 2 celery stalks, diced
- 1 bell pepper, diced
- 8 ounces (about 225g) mushrooms, chopped
- 1 can (15 ounces) lentils, drained and rinsed (or 1 1/2 cups cooked lentils)
- 1 cup frozen peas
- 1 tablespoon tomato paste
- 1 tablespoon soy sauce or tamari
- 1 teaspoon dried thyme
- 1 teaspoon dried rosemary
- Salt and pepper, to taste
- 1/2 cup vegetable broth or water

Instructions:

1. **Make the Mashed Potatoes:**
   - Place the chopped potatoes in a large pot and cover with water. Bring to a boil over high heat, then reduce the heat to medium and simmer for 15-20 minutes, or until the potatoes are tender when pierced with a fork.
   - Drain the potatoes and return them to the pot. Add almond milk, vegan butter, salt, and pepper. Mash the potatoes until smooth and creamy. Set aside.
2. **Prepare the Filling:**
   - Preheat the oven to 375°F (190°C).

- In a large skillet, heat olive oil over medium heat. Add chopped onion and sauté for 5-7 minutes until translucent.
   - Add minced garlic, diced carrots, diced celery, diced bell pepper, and chopped mushrooms to the skillet. Cook for another 5-7 minutes until the vegetables are tender.
3. **Add Lentils and Seasonings:**
   - Stir in drained and rinsed lentils, frozen peas, tomato paste, soy sauce or tamari, dried thyme, dried rosemary, salt, and pepper. Cook for 2-3 minutes, stirring frequently.
4. **Add Liquid and Simmer:**
   - Pour in vegetable broth or water and bring the mixture to a simmer. Let it cook for 5-7 minutes, stirring occasionally, until the liquid has reduced and the filling is thickened. Adjust seasoning if needed.
5. **Assemble the Shepherd's Pie:**
   - Transfer the lentil and vegetable mixture to a baking dish (9x13 inches or similar size). Spread it out evenly.
   - Spoon the mashed potatoes over the filling, spreading them to cover the entire surface. Use a fork to create a decorative pattern on the top if desired.
6. **Bake:**
   - Place the assembled Shepherd's Pie in the preheated oven and bake for 25-30 minutes, or until the top is golden brown and the filling is bubbling around the edges.
7. **Serve:**
   - Remove from the oven and let it cool for a few minutes before serving.
   - Garnish with chopped fresh herbs like parsley or thyme if desired.
8. **Enjoy:**
   - Serve the vegan Shepherd's Pie warm, portioned out as a delicious and satisfying main dish.

This vegan Shepherd's Pie is packed with flavor and wholesome ingredients, making it a perfect comforting meal for any occasion. Adjust the seasonings and vegetables based on your preferences, and enjoy this hearty dish with family and friends!

Cauliflower Mashed Potatoes

Ingredients:

- 1 medium head of cauliflower, cut into florets
- 2-3 cloves garlic, peeled
- 2 tablespoons vegan butter or olive oil
- 1/4 cup unsweetened almond milk or other non-dairy milk
- Salt and pepper, to taste
- Chopped fresh chives or parsley, for garnish (optional)

Instructions:

1. **Steam the Cauliflower:**
   - Bring a large pot of water to a boil. Place the cauliflower florets and garlic cloves in a steamer basket or directly in the boiling water. Steam for about 10-12 minutes, or until the cauliflower is very tender when pierced with a fork.
2. **Mash the Cauliflower:**
   - Drain the cauliflower and garlic. Transfer them to a large mixing bowl or food processor.
   - Add vegan butter or olive oil, almond milk, salt, and pepper to taste.
3. **Blend or Mash:**
   - If using a food processor, pulse until the cauliflower is smooth and creamy. If mashing by hand, use a potato masher or fork to mash until desired consistency is reached. Add more almond milk if needed to achieve desired creaminess.
4. **Adjust Seasoning:**
   - Taste and adjust seasoning with more salt and pepper if necessary.
5. **Serve:**
   - Transfer the cauliflower mashed potatoes to a serving bowl.
   - Garnish with chopped fresh chives or parsley if desired.
6. **Enjoy:**
   - Serve the cauliflower mashed potatoes warm as a delicious and nutritious side dish alongside your favorite main course.

Tips:

- **Variations:** You can add nutritional yeast for a cheesy flavor or roasted garlic for extra depth of flavor.

- **Texture:** For a smoother texture, blend the cauliflower mixture longer in the food processor.
- **Storage:** Leftovers can be stored in an airtight container in the refrigerator for up to 3 days. Reheat gently on the stovetop or in the microwave before serving.

This vegan cauliflower mashed potatoes recipe is creamy, flavorful, and a great alternative to traditional mashed potatoes. It's perfect for holiday meals or anytime you want a lighter, veggie-packed side dish.

Garlic Rosemary Roasted Potatoes

Ingredients:

- 2 lbs (about 1 kg) baby potatoes, halved or quartered depending on size
- 3-4 cloves garlic, minced
- 2-3 tablespoons olive oil
- 2-3 tablespoons fresh rosemary, chopped (or 1 tablespoon dried rosemary)
- Salt and pepper, to taste
- Lemon zest (optional), for garnish

Instructions:

1. **Preheat the Oven:**
   - Preheat your oven to 400°F (200°C).
2. **Prepare the Potatoes:**
   - Wash and scrub the baby potatoes thoroughly. If they are larger, halve or quarter them so they cook evenly.
3. **Season the Potatoes:**
   - In a large bowl, toss the potatoes with minced garlic, olive oil, chopped fresh rosemary (or dried rosemary), salt, and pepper. Mix well until the potatoes are evenly coated with the seasonings.
4. **Roast the Potatoes:**
   - Spread the seasoned potatoes in a single layer on a large baking sheet lined with parchment paper or lightly greased.
   - Roast in the preheated oven for 30-35 minutes, or until the potatoes are golden brown and crispy on the outside, and tender on the inside. Stir or shake the pan halfway through cooking to ensure even browning.
5. **Garnish and Serve:**
   - Remove from the oven and transfer the roasted potatoes to a serving dish.
   - Optional: Garnish with a sprinkle of fresh lemon zest for an extra burst of flavor.
6. **Enjoy:**
   - Serve the garlic rosemary roasted potatoes hot as a delicious side dish alongside your favorite main course.

Tips:

- **Variations:** Add other herbs like thyme or sage for additional flavor. You can also toss in some diced onions or bell peppers for added color and taste.

- **Crispiness:** For extra crispy potatoes, turn on the broiler for the last 1-2 minutes of cooking, keeping a close eye to prevent burning.
- **Storage:** Leftover roasted potatoes can be stored in an airtight container in the refrigerator for up to 3 days. Reheat in the oven or toaster oven for best results.

These garlic rosemary roasted potatoes are simple to make yet packed with flavor, making them a versatile and satisfying addition to any meal. Enjoy them as a side dish for holidays, gatherings, or any day of the week!

Baked Apples with Cinnamon

Ingredients:

- 4 medium apples (such as Granny Smith or Honeycrisp)
- 2 tablespoons maple syrup or agave syrup
- 1 teaspoon ground cinnamon
- 1/4 teaspoon ground nutmeg
- 1/4 cup chopped nuts (such as walnuts or pecans), optional
- Vegan vanilla ice cream or coconut whipped cream, for serving (optional)

Instructions:

1. **Preheat the Oven:**
   - Preheat your oven to 375°F (190°C).
2. **Prepare the Apples:**
   - Wash the apples and remove the cores using an apple corer or a small knife, leaving the bottom intact. This creates a well for the filling.
3. **Make the Filling:**
   - In a small bowl, mix together maple syrup or agave syrup, ground cinnamon, and ground nutmeg until well combined.
4. **Fill the Apples:**
   - Place the cored apples in a baking dish. Spoon the cinnamon mixture evenly into each apple, allowing it to fill the cavity. If using chopped nuts, sprinkle them over the top of each apple.
5. **Bake the Apples:**
   - Bake in the preheated oven for 25-30 minutes, or until the apples are tender and the filling is bubbly and caramelized.
6. **Serve:**
   - Remove the baked apples from the oven and let them cool slightly.
   - Serve warm, optionally topped with vegan vanilla ice cream or coconut whipped cream.
7. **Enjoy:**
   - Enjoy these delicious baked apples with cinnamon as a comforting dessert or snack.

Tips:

- **Variations:** Add dried fruit like raisins or cranberries to the filling for extra sweetness and texture.

- **Nuts:** If using nuts, you can also mix them into the cinnamon filling before spooning it into the apples.
- **Storage:** Baked apples are best served fresh and warm. If you have leftovers, store them in an airtight container in the refrigerator and reheat gently before serving.

This vegan baked apples with cinnamon recipe is simple yet flavorful, showcasing the natural sweetness of apples enhanced by warm spices. It's perfect for any occasion and can be enjoyed guilt-free as a healthier dessert option.

Vegan Pecan Pie

Ingredients:

For the Pie Crust:

- 1 1/4 cups all-purpose flour
- 1/2 cup vegan butter, chilled and cut into small cubes
- 1/4 teaspoon salt
- 2-4 tablespoons ice water

For the Pecan Filling:

- 1 1/2 cups pecan halves
- 1 cup full-fat coconut milk (from a can)
- 3/4 cup brown sugar or coconut sugar
- 1/4 cup maple syrup
- 2 tablespoons cornstarch or arrowroot powder
- 1 teaspoon vanilla extract
- 1/4 teaspoon salt

Instructions:

For the Pie Crust:

1. **Prepare the Crust:**
    - In a large bowl, whisk together the flour and salt. Add the chilled vegan butter cubes.
    - Use a pastry cutter or fork to cut the butter into the flour until the mixture resembles coarse crumbs.
    - Gradually add ice water, one tablespoon at a time, mixing with a fork, until the dough begins to come together.
    - Shape the dough into a ball, flatten into a disc, wrap in plastic wrap, and refrigerate for at least 30 minutes.
2. **Roll Out the Crust:**
    - Preheat your oven to 375°F (190°C).
    - On a lightly floured surface, roll out the chilled dough into a circle about 12 inches in diameter.
    - Carefully transfer the rolled-out dough to a 9-inch pie dish. Press the dough into the bottom and sides of the dish. Trim any excess dough and crimp the edges as desired.

3. **Pre-bake the Crust (optional):**
   - To prevent a soggy bottom crust, you can pre-bake the crust. Line the pie crust with parchment paper or aluminum foil and fill with pie weights or dried beans.
   - Bake in the preheated oven for 15 minutes. Remove the weights and parchment/foil, then bake for another 5 minutes until lightly golden. Remove from the oven and set aside.

For the Pecan Filling:

4. **Prepare the Filling:**
   - In a medium bowl, whisk together coconut milk, brown sugar or coconut sugar, maple syrup, cornstarch or arrowroot powder, vanilla extract, and salt until smooth and well combined.
5. **Assemble the Pie:**
   - Arrange pecan halves evenly over the pre-baked pie crust.
   - Pour the coconut milk mixture evenly over the pecans, ensuring they are well coated.
6. **Bake the Pie:**
   - Place the pie in the preheated oven and bake for 45-50 minutes, or until the filling is set and the edges of the crust are golden brown. If the crust edges start to brown too quickly, you can cover them with aluminum foil halfway through baking.
7. **Cool and Serve:**
   - Allow the pie to cool completely on a wire rack before slicing and serving.
   - Serve slices of vegan pecan pie on its own or with a dollop of vegan whipped cream or vanilla ice cream.

Tips:

- **Storage:** Leftover pie can be stored in an airtight container at room temperature for up to 2 days, or in the refrigerator for up to 5 days.
- **Crust Options:** If you prefer, you can use a store-bought vegan pie crust to save time.
- **Nut-Free Option:** If you have a nut allergy, you can substitute pecans with seeds like pumpkin seeds or sunflower seeds for a different texture.

This vegan pecan pie recipe captures all the flavors and textures you love about traditional pecan pie while being completely plant-based. It's perfect for holidays, special occasions, or any time you crave a decadent dessert without animal products. Enjoy!

Chocolate Avocado Mousse

Ingredients:

- 2 ripe avocados
- 1/3 cup cocoa powder (unsweetened)
- 1/3 cup maple syrup or agave syrup (adjust to taste)
- 1 teaspoon vanilla extract
- Pinch of salt
- Optional toppings: shaved chocolate, berries, nuts, or coconut flakes

Instructions:

1. **Prepare the Avocados:**
   - Cut the avocados in half, remove the pits, and scoop the flesh into a food processor or blender.
2. **Blend Ingredients:**
   - Add cocoa powder, maple syrup or agave syrup, vanilla extract, and a pinch of salt to the avocados in the food processor or blender.
3. **Blend Until Smooth:**
   - Blend the ingredients until smooth and creamy, scraping down the sides of the bowl as needed to ensure everything is well combined. Taste and adjust sweetness if necessary by adding more maple syrup or agave syrup.
4. **Chill (optional):**
   - For a thicker consistency, chill the mousse in the refrigerator for at least 30 minutes before serving.
5. **Serve:**
   - Divide the chocolate avocado mousse into serving dishes.
   - Optionally, top with shaved chocolate, berries, nuts, or coconut flakes for added texture and flavor.
6. **Enjoy:**
   - Serve immediately and enjoy this deliciously creamy chocolate avocado mousse!

Tips:

- **Ripeness of Avocados:** Make sure your avocados are ripe but not overripe. They should be soft enough to blend smoothly.

- **Sweetness:** Adjust the sweetness according to your taste preferences. You can also use other sweeteners like date syrup or honey (if not strictly vegan).
- **Texture:** If you prefer a lighter mousse, you can add a few tablespoons of coconut milk or almond milk while blending.

This chocolate avocado mousse is not only vegan and dairy-free but also packed with healthy fats from avocados and antioxidants from cocoa powder. It's a guilt-free dessert that satisfies chocolate cravings while offering nutritional benefits. Enjoy it as a dessert or a special treat any time!

Holiday Fruit Salad

Ingredients:

- 2 cups fresh strawberries, hulled and sliced
- 2 cups fresh pineapple, diced
- 2 cups fresh mandarin oranges, peeled and segmented
- 1 cup red grapes, halved
- 1 cup green grapes, halved
- 1 cup pomegranate arils (seeds)
- 1/4 cup fresh mint leaves, thinly sliced (optional, for garnish)

For the Dressing:

- 1/4 cup freshly squeezed orange juice
- 2 tablespoons maple syrup or agave syrup
- 1 tablespoon lemon juice
- Zest of 1 orange (optional, for extra flavor)

Instructions:

1. **Prepare the Fruit:**
   - Wash and prepare all the fruits as instructed (slice, dice, peel, etc.). Place them in a large mixing bowl.
2. **Make the Dressing:**
   - In a small bowl, whisk together the orange juice, maple syrup or agave syrup, lemon juice, and orange zest (if using) until well combined.
3. **Combine Fruit and Dressing:**
   - Pour the dressing over the prepared fruits in the large mixing bowl.
4. **Gently Toss:**
   - Gently toss the fruits with the dressing until they are evenly coated.
5. **Chill:**
   - Cover the bowl with plastic wrap or transfer the fruit salad to a sealed container. Refrigerate for at least 30 minutes to allow the flavors to meld together.
6. **Serve:**
   - Before serving, give the fruit salad a gentle toss again to redistribute the dressing.
   - Garnish with thinly sliced fresh mint leaves if desired.
7. **Enjoy:**

- Serve the holiday fruit salad chilled as a refreshing and colorful side dish or dessert.

Tips:

- **Variations:** Feel free to add other seasonal fruits such as apples, kiwi, mango, or berries depending on availability and your preferences.
- **Make Ahead:** You can prepare the fruit and dressing separately up to a day in advance and combine them just before serving to keep the fruits fresh.
- **Sweetness:** Adjust the sweetness of the dressing by adding more or less maple syrup/agave syrup according to your taste and the sweetness of the fruits.

This vegan holiday fruit salad is not only beautiful to look at but also packed with vitamins, fiber, and natural sweetness from fresh fruits. It's a perfect addition to your holiday table, providing a light and refreshing contrast to richer dishes.

Vegan Eggnog

Ingredients:

- 2 cups unsweetened almond milk (or any other non-dairy milk of choice)
- 1 cup canned coconut milk (full-fat for creaminess)
- 1/4 cup maple syrup or agave syrup (adjust to taste)
- 1 teaspoon vanilla extract
- 1/2 teaspoon ground cinnamon
- 1/2 teaspoon ground nutmeg
- 1/4 teaspoon ground cloves
- Pinch of salt
- Optional: 1/4 cup bourbon, rum, or brandy (for a spiked version, adjust to taste)
- Cinnamon sticks or ground cinnamon, for garnish
- Ground nutmeg, for garnish

Instructions:

1. **Blend Ingredients:**
   - In a blender, combine unsweetened almond milk, canned coconut milk, maple syrup or agave syrup, vanilla extract, ground cinnamon, ground nutmeg, ground cloves, and a pinch of salt.
2. **Blend Until Smooth:**
   - Blend the ingredients until smooth and well combined.
3. **Add Alcohol (optional):**
   - If making a spiked version, add bourbon, rum, or brandy to the blender and blend again until mixed thoroughly.
4. **Chill:**
   - Transfer the eggnog mixture to a pitcher or container and refrigerate for at least 2 hours, or until chilled. Chilling allows the flavors to meld together.
5. **Serve:**
   - Before serving, stir the eggnog well. Pour into glasses and garnish with a sprinkle of ground nutmeg and a cinnamon stick or sprinkle of ground cinnamon on top.
6. **Enjoy:**
   - Serve the vegan eggnog chilled and enjoy its creamy, spiced goodness.

Tips:

- **Sweetness:** Adjust the sweetness by adding more maple syrup or agave syrup if desired.
- **Thickness:** For a thicker eggnog, you can use more canned coconut milk or add a tablespoon of cornstarch mixed with water and heated until thickened.
- **Variations:** Experiment with different spices such as cardamom or allspice for added flavor complexity.
- **Storage:** Leftover eggnog can be stored in the refrigerator for up to 3-4 days. Stir well before serving as it may separate slightly.

This vegan eggnog recipe is a wonderful dairy-free alternative that captures the festive flavors of traditional eggnog. It's perfect for serving at holiday parties or enjoying by the fire on a chilly evening. Cheers!

Gingerbread Cookies

Ingredients:

- 3 cups all-purpose flour
- 1 teaspoon baking soda
- 1/2 teaspoon baking powder
- 1/2 teaspoon salt
- 1 tablespoon ground ginger
- 1 teaspoon ground cinnamon
- 1/4 teaspoon ground cloves
- 1/4 teaspoon ground nutmeg
- 1/2 cup vegan butter, softened (such as Earth Balance)
- 1/2 cup brown sugar, packed
- 1/2 cup molasses
- 1 tablespoon ground flaxseed meal + 3 tablespoons water (or use a commercial egg replacer)
- 1 teaspoon vanilla extract

Instructions:

1. **Prepare Flaxseed Egg:**
    - In a small bowl, mix ground flaxseed meal with water. Let it sit for 5 minutes to thicken and form a "flax egg."
2. **Prepare the Dough:**
    - In a medium bowl, whisk together flour, baking soda, baking powder, salt, ginger, cinnamon, cloves, and nutmeg until well combined.
3. **Cream Butter and Sugar:**
    - In a large mixing bowl, cream together softened vegan butter and brown sugar using a hand mixer or stand mixer, until light and fluffy.
4. **Add Molasses and Flaxseed Egg:**
    - Add molasses, vanilla extract, and the prepared flaxseed egg to the creamed butter and sugar. Mix until well combined.
5. **Combine Wet and Dry Ingredients:**
    - Gradually add the dry ingredient mixture to the wet ingredients, mixing on low speed until a dough forms. If the dough seems too sticky, add a little more flour, 1 tablespoon at a time.
6. **Chill the Dough:**

- Divide the dough into two equal portions and flatten each into a disc. Wrap each disc tightly in plastic wrap and refrigerate for at least 1 hour, or until firm.

7. **Preheat Oven:**
    - Preheat your oven to 350°F (175°C) and line baking sheets with parchment paper.
8. **Roll Out and Cut Cookies:**
    - On a lightly floured surface, roll out one disc of chilled dough to about 1/4 inch thickness. Use cookie cutters to cut out shapes and transfer them to the prepared baking sheets, spacing them about 1 inch apart.
9. **Bake:**
    - Bake the cookies in the preheated oven for 8-10 minutes, or until the edges are firm and lightly browned. Be careful not to overbake.
10. **Cool and Decorate:**
    - Remove the cookies from the oven and let them cool on the baking sheets for a few minutes before transferring them to wire racks to cool completely.
    - Once cooled, decorate the cookies with icing or enjoy them plain.
11. **Enjoy:**
    - Serve and enjoy these delicious vegan gingerbread cookies!

Tips:

- **Icing:** You can decorate your gingerbread cookies with vegan royal icing or a simple glaze made with powdered sugar and non-dairy milk.
- **Storage:** Store cooled cookies in an airtight container at room temperature for up to one week, or freeze them for longer storage.

These vegan gingerbread cookies are perfect for holiday gatherings, cookie exchanges, or simply as a festive treat to enjoy with a cup of hot cocoa or tea. They are flavorful, aromatic, and sure to be a hit with vegans and non-vegans alike!

Mulled Wine

Ingredients:

- 1 bottle (750 ml) red wine (choose a vegan-friendly variety)
- 1 orange, thinly sliced
- 1/4 cup maple syrup or agave syrup (adjust to taste)
- 1 cinnamon stick
- 6 whole cloves
- 3 whole star anise
- Optional: 1/4 cup brandy or rum (for a spiked version)

Instructions:

1. **Prepare the Spices:**
   - In a small saucepan, combine the orange slices, cinnamon stick, whole cloves, and star anise.
2. **Simmer the Spices:**
   - Pour in enough red wine to cover the spices (about 1 cup). Simmer over medium-low heat for 10-15 minutes to infuse the flavors into the wine. This step helps to release the aromas and flavors of the spices.
3. **Add Remaining Ingredients:**
   - Pour the remaining red wine into the saucepan. Add maple syrup or agave syrup and stir to combine.
4. **Heat Gently:**
   - Heat the mulled wine mixture over low heat, stirring occasionally. Be careful not to let it boil, as this can cause the alcohol to evaporate.
5. **Steep and Infuse:**
   - Allow the mulled wine to steep and infuse with the flavors of the spices for at least 15-20 minutes. The longer you steep it, the more pronounced the flavors will be.
6. **Strain and Serve:**
   - Remove the mulled wine from heat and strain out the spices and orange slices. Discard the spices.
7. **Serve Warm:**
   - Ladle the warm mulled wine into mugs or heatproof glasses.
8. **Optional:**
   - You can add a splash of brandy or rum to each serving for a spiked version of mulled wine, if desired.

9. **Garnish:**
    - Garnish each glass with a cinnamon stick or a slice of orange, if desired.
10. **Enjoy:**
    - Serve and enjoy your vegan mulled wine while it's warm and aromatic!

Tips:

- **Wine Selection:** Choose a red wine that you enjoy drinking. Traditional choices include Merlot, Cabernet Sauvignon, or Zinfandel.
- **Sweetness:** Adjust the sweetness to your taste by adding more or less maple syrup or agave syrup.
- **Variations:** Feel free to customize your mulled wine with additional spices such as cardamom pods, ginger slices, or a dash of ground nutmeg for extra flavor complexity.

This vegan mulled wine recipe is perfect for cozy evenings and festive gatherings, offering a comforting blend of warm spices and red wine. It's a delightful drink to enjoy with friends and family during the holiday season or anytime you want to warm up on a chilly day. Cheers!

Roasted Brussels Sprouts with Balsamic Glaze

Ingredients:

- 1 lb Brussels sprouts, trimmed and halved
- 2 tablespoons olive oil
- Salt and pepper, to taste
- 2-3 tablespoons balsamic vinegar
- 1-2 tablespoons maple syrup or agave syrup (optional, for sweetness)
- 1-2 cloves garlic, minced (optional, for extra flavor)
- 2 tablespoons chopped walnuts or pecans (optional, for garnish)

Instructions:

1. **Preheat the Oven:**
    - Preheat your oven to 400°F (200°C).
2. **Prepare Brussels Sprouts:**
    - Trim the ends of the Brussels sprouts and cut them in half lengthwise. Remove any outer leaves that are yellow or wilted.
3. **Toss with Olive Oil and Seasoning:**
    - In a large bowl, toss the halved Brussels sprouts with olive oil, salt, and pepper until evenly coated.
4. **Roast Brussels Sprouts:**
    - Spread the Brussels sprouts in a single layer on a baking sheet lined with parchment paper or aluminum foil. Roast in the preheated oven for 20-25 minutes, or until they are golden brown and crispy on the edges, tossing halfway through for even cooking.
5. **Prepare Balsamic Glaze:**
    - While the Brussels sprouts are roasting, prepare the balsamic glaze. In a small saucepan, heat balsamic vinegar over medium heat until it starts to simmer. If using, add maple syrup or agave syrup and minced garlic. Stir occasionally and simmer for 5-7 minutes, or until the glaze thickens slightly. Remove from heat.
6. **Combine and Serve:**
    - Remove the roasted Brussels sprouts from the oven and transfer them to a serving dish.
    - Drizzle the balsamic glaze over the roasted Brussels sprouts and toss gently to coat.
7. **Garnish (optional):**

- If desired, garnish with chopped walnuts or pecans for added texture and flavor.
8. **Enjoy:**
   - Serve the roasted Brussels sprouts with balsamic glaze immediately as a delicious and nutritious side dish.

Tips:

- **Variations:** Feel free to add other seasonings such as smoked paprika, thyme, or rosemary to the Brussels sprouts before roasting for different flavor profiles.
- **Sweetness:** Adjust the sweetness of the balsamic glaze to your taste preference. Some balsamic vinegars are naturally sweeter than others.
- **Storage:** Leftover roasted Brussels sprouts can be stored in an airtight container in the refrigerator for up to 3 days. Reheat gently in the oven or microwave before serving.

This recipe for roasted Brussels sprouts with balsamic glaze is simple yet incredibly flavorful, making it a perfect side dish for holiday meals or everyday dinners. It's sure to become a favorite among vegans and non-vegans alike!

Vegan Tiramisu

Ingredients:

For the Cashew Mascarpone:

- 1 1/2 cups raw cashews, soaked in water for at least 4 hours or overnight
- 1/2 cup full-fat coconut milk (from a can)
- 1/4 cup maple syrup or agave syrup
- 2 tablespoons lemon juice
- 1 teaspoon vanilla extract

For the Espresso Soaking Liquid:

- 1 cup strong brewed coffee or espresso, cooled
- 2 tablespoons maple syrup or agave syrup
- 2 tablespoons coffee liqueur (optional)

For Assembling:

- 1 package (about 7 ounces) vegan ladyfingers (savoiardi)
- Cocoa powder, for dusting
- Dark chocolate shavings or cocoa nibs, for garnish (optional)

Instructions:

1. **Prepare the Cashew Mascarpone:**
    - Drain and rinse the soaked cashews.
    - In a high-speed blender or food processor, combine the soaked cashews, coconut milk, maple syrup or agave syrup, lemon juice, and vanilla extract.
    - Blend until smooth and creamy, scraping down the sides as needed. The consistency should be similar to a thick cream cheese. If too thick, add a tablespoon of coconut milk at a time to achieve the desired consistency.
2. **Prepare the Espresso Soaking Liquid:**
    - In a shallow dish, whisk together the cooled brewed coffee or espresso with maple syrup or agave syrup and coffee liqueur (if using). Set aside.
3. **Assemble the Tiramisu:**
    - Dip each vegan ladyfinger into the espresso soaking liquid for a few seconds on each side. Be careful not to soak them too long, as they can become soggy quickly.

- Arrange a layer of soaked ladyfingers in the bottom of an 8x8 inch baking dish or a similar-sized serving dish.
- Spread half of the cashew mascarpone mixture evenly over the soaked ladyfingers.
- Dust with cocoa powder using a fine mesh sieve.

4. **Repeat the Layers:**
   - Repeat the layers with another layer of soaked ladyfingers, the remaining cashew mascarpone mixture, and a final dusting of cocoa powder.

5. **Chill and Set:**
   - Cover the tiramisu with plastic wrap and refrigerate for at least 4 hours, preferably overnight, to allow the flavors to meld and the dessert to set.

6. **Garnish and Serve:**
   - Before serving, garnish with dark chocolate shavings or cocoa nibs, if desired.
   - Slice and serve chilled. Enjoy your delicious vegan tiramisu!

Tips:

- **Ladyfingers:** Look for vegan ladyfingers (savoiardi) in specialty stores or online. They should be crisp and absorbent to soak up the espresso mixture.
- **Storage:** Vegan tiramisu can be stored covered in the refrigerator for up to 3 days. It actually tastes better as it sits, allowing the flavors to meld together.
- **Alcohol-Free Option:** If you prefer an alcohol-free version, omit the coffee liqueur from the soaking liquid.

This vegan tiramisu recipe captures the essence of the classic dessert with a dairy-free twist, making it a perfect indulgence for those following a plant-based diet or anyone looking for a delicious dessert option. Enjoy the creamy layers and rich flavors of this vegan treat!

Pomegranate Salad

Ingredients:

- 4 cups mixed salad greens (such as baby spinach, arugula, or mixed greens)
- 1 cup pomegranate arils (seeds)
- 1/2 cup walnut halves, toasted
- 1/4 cup red onion, thinly sliced
- 1/4 cup fresh parsley, chopped
- 1/4 cup fresh mint leaves, chopped
- 1/4 cup vegan feta cheese, crumbled (optional)

For the Dressing:

- 3 tablespoons extra virgin olive oil
- 2 tablespoons balsamic vinegar
- 1 tablespoon maple syrup or agave syrup
- 1 teaspoon Dijon mustard
- Salt and pepper, to taste

Instructions:

1. **Prepare the Salad Greens:**
    - Wash and dry the mixed salad greens thoroughly. Place them in a large salad bowl.
2. **Toast the Walnuts:**
    - In a dry skillet over medium heat, toast the walnut halves for 3-5 minutes, stirring frequently, until fragrant and lightly browned. Remove from heat and let them cool.
3. **Prepare the Dressing:**
    - In a small bowl, whisk together extra virgin olive oil, balsamic vinegar, maple syrup or agave syrup, Dijon mustard, salt, and pepper until well combined.
4. **Assemble the Salad:**
    - Add the pomegranate arils, toasted walnuts, sliced red onion, chopped parsley, and chopped mint leaves to the salad greens.
5. **Add the Dressing:**
    - Drizzle the dressing over the salad ingredients in the bowl. Toss gently to coat all the ingredients evenly with the dressing.
6. **Optional:**

- If using vegan feta cheese, sprinkle it over the salad just before serving.
7. **Serve:**
   - Serve the pomegranate salad immediately as a refreshing and colorful side dish or main course.

Tips:

- **Pomegranate Preparation:** To easily remove the arils from the pomegranate, cut it in half and gently tap the back with a wooden spoon over a bowl to release the seeds.
- **Variations:** Feel free to add other ingredients such as avocado slices, cucumber slices, or cooked quinoa for added texture and flavor.
- **Make Ahead:** You can prepare the dressing and toast the walnuts in advance. Assemble the salad just before serving to keep the greens crisp.

This vegan pomegranate salad is bursting with flavors, textures, and nutrients, making it a perfect dish for holidays, special occasions, or everyday meals. Enjoy the sweet-tart crunch of pomegranate arils paired with fresh greens and a tangy balsamic dressing!

Stuffed Portobello Mushrooms

Ingredients:

- 4 large portobello mushrooms, stems removed
- 1 tablespoon olive oil
- 1 small onion, finely chopped
- 2 cloves garlic, minced
- 1 cup baby spinach, chopped
- 1/2 cup sun-dried tomatoes, chopped
- 1/2 cup breadcrumbs (use gluten-free breadcrumbs if needed)
- 1/4 cup nutritional yeast
- 1/4 cup fresh basil, chopped
- Salt and pepper, to taste
- Vegan cheese (optional, for topping)

Instructions:

1. **Prepare the Portobello Mushrooms:**
   - Preheat the oven to 375°F (190°C). Line a baking sheet with parchment paper.
   - Remove the stems from the portobello mushrooms and gently scrape out the gills using a spoon. Place the mushrooms on the prepared baking sheet with the cap side down.
2. **Prepare the Filling:**
   - In a large skillet, heat olive oil over medium heat. Add chopped onion and garlic, sautéing until softened and fragrant, about 3-4 minutes.
   - Add chopped spinach and sun-dried tomatoes to the skillet. Cook for another 2-3 minutes until the spinach is wilted.
3. **Combine the Ingredients:**
   - Remove the skillet from heat. Stir in breadcrumbs, nutritional yeast, chopped basil, salt, and pepper. Mix until well combined and the filling holds together.
4. **Stuff the Mushrooms:**
   - Spoon the filling mixture evenly into each portobello mushroom cap, pressing gently to pack it in.
5. **Bake the Stuffed Mushrooms:**
   - Bake in the preheated oven for 20-25 minutes, or until the mushrooms are tender and the filling is golden brown on top.

6. **Optional:**
    - If using vegan cheese, sprinkle it over the stuffed mushrooms during the last 5 minutes of baking until melted and bubbly.
7. **Serve:**
    - Remove the stuffed portobello mushrooms from the oven and let them cool slightly before serving. Garnish with additional fresh basil if desired.

Tips:

- **Variations:** Feel free to customize the filling with other vegetables or herbs such as diced bell peppers, artichoke hearts, or thyme.
- **Make Ahead:** You can prepare the filling in advance and store it in the refrigerator. Stuff the mushrooms and bake them when ready to serve.
- **Serve With:** Stuffed portobello mushrooms pair well with a side salad or roasted vegetables for a complete meal.

These vegan stuffed portobello mushrooms are packed with flavor and make a satisfying dish that will please vegans and non-vegans alike. Enjoy them as a delicious appetizer or main course for a hearty and nutritious meal!

Vegan Truffles

Ingredients:

- 1 cup vegan chocolate chips or chopped dark chocolate
- 1/2 cup full-fat coconut milk (from a can)
- 1 teaspoon vanilla extract
- Pinch of salt
- Cocoa powder, shredded coconut, crushed nuts, or melted chocolate (for coating)

Optional Additions for Flavor Variations:

- 1-2 tablespoons almond butter or peanut butter
- 1-2 tablespoons maple syrup or agave syrup (for added sweetness)

Instructions:

1. **Prepare the Ganache:**
   - In a small saucepan, heat the coconut milk over medium heat until it starts to simmer (do not boil).
   - Remove from heat and add the vegan chocolate chips or chopped chocolate to the saucepan. Let it sit for 1-2 minutes to soften.
2. **Mix and Melt:**
   - Stir the chocolate and coconut milk together until smooth and well combined. If needed, return the saucepan to low heat and continue stirring until completely melted and smooth.
   - Stir in vanilla extract, salt, and any optional additions like almond butter or maple syrup, if using. Mix until fully incorporated.
3. **Chill the Mixture:**
   - Transfer the chocolate mixture (ganache) to a bowl and let it cool to room temperature. Then, cover the bowl and refrigerate for at least 2 hours, or until the mixture is firm enough to handle and roll into balls.
4. **Shape the Truffles:**
   - Once chilled, use a spoon or a small cookie scoop to scoop out portions of the chilled ganache mixture. Roll each portion between your palms to form smooth balls.
5. **Coat the Truffles:**

- Roll each truffle in cocoa powder, shredded coconut, crushed nuts, or dip them in melted chocolate to coat evenly. Place them on a parchment-lined baking sheet.
6. **Chill and Set:**
    - Once coated, refrigerate the truffles for another 15-20 minutes to allow the coatings to set.
7. **Serve and Enjoy:**
    - Arrange the vegan truffles on a serving plate or in small candy cups.
    - Store any leftovers in an airtight container in the refrigerator for up to 1 week. Bring to room temperature before serving.

Tips:

- **Chocolate:** Use high-quality vegan chocolate for the best flavor and texture.
- **Consistency:** If the ganache mixture is too soft to roll into balls, refrigerate it for a bit longer until firm enough.
- **Variations:** Experiment with different coatings such as matcha powder, finely chopped dried fruit, or sprinkles for added texture and flavor.

These vegan truffles are a delightful treat that's sure to impress with their creamy, chocolatey goodness. Whether you're making them for a special occasion or as a homemade gift, they're bound to be a hit!

Roasted Chestnuts

Ingredients:

- Fresh chestnuts (as many as you like)
- Water

Instructions:

1. **Preheat the Oven:**
    - Preheat your oven to 425°F (220°C).
2. **Prepare the Chestnuts:**
    - Using a sharp knife, carefully score an "X" on the flat side of each chestnut. This allows steam to escape and prevents them from bursting during roasting.
3. **Soak the Chestnuts (optional):**
    - Some people prefer to soak the scored chestnuts in water for about 10-15 minutes before roasting. This can help make them easier to peel after roasting, but it's optional.
4. **Roast the Chestnuts:**
    - Arrange the scored and optionally soaked chestnuts in a single layer on a baking sheet lined with parchment paper or aluminum foil, flat side down.
5. **Roast in the Oven:**
    - Roast the chestnuts in the preheated oven for 15-20 minutes. The exact timing will depend on the size of the chestnuts and your oven. They should be tender and the scored shells should start to peel back.
6. **Cool Slightly:**
    - Remove the chestnuts from the oven and let them cool slightly until they are cool enough to handle but still warm.
7. **Peel and Enjoy:**
    - While the chestnuts are still warm, peel away the outer shell and the thin inner skin (pellicle). This is easiest to do while they are still warm.
8. **Serve:**
    - Enjoy the roasted chestnuts warm as a snack, appetizer, or use them in recipes like stuffing or desserts.

Tips:

- **Handling Chestnuts:** Be careful when handling hot chestnuts, as they can be quite hot immediately after roasting.

- **Storage:** Roasted chestnuts are best enjoyed fresh. If you have leftovers, store them in an airtight container in the refrigerator and consume within a few days.

Roasting chestnuts at home is a delightful experience, filling your kitchen with a wonderful aroma and providing a delicious snack that's perfect for chilly evenings or festive gatherings. Enjoy the warm, nutty flavor of freshly roasted chestnuts!

Spinach Artichoke Dip

Ingredients:

- 1 tablespoon olive oil
- 3 cloves garlic, minced
- 1 small onion, finely chopped
- 1 can (14 oz) artichoke hearts, drained and chopped
- 4 cups fresh spinach, chopped
- 1 cup raw cashews, soaked in hot water for 1 hour or in cold water overnight
- 1 cup vegetable broth
- 1/4 cup nutritional yeast
- 1/4 cup vegan mayonnaise
- 1 tablespoon lemon juice
- 1 teaspoon onion powder
- 1/2 teaspoon garlic powder
- Salt and pepper, to taste
- Red pepper flakes (optional, for a bit of heat)
- Vegan shredded mozzarella or Parmesan cheese (optional, for topping)

Instructions:

1. **Prepare the Cashews:**
   - If you haven't already soaked the cashews, place them in a bowl and cover with hot water. Let them soak for 1 hour, then drain and rinse.
2. **Sauté Vegetables:**
   - In a large skillet, heat olive oil over medium heat. Add minced garlic and chopped onion. Sauté until the onions are translucent and garlic is fragrant, about 3-4 minutes.
3. **Add Spinach and Artichokes:**
   - Add chopped artichoke hearts to the skillet and cook for another 2-3 minutes until heated through. Add chopped spinach and cook until wilted, about 2 minutes. Remove from heat and set aside.
4. **Blend Cashew Cream:**
   - In a blender, combine soaked and drained cashews, vegetable broth, nutritional yeast, vegan mayonnaise, lemon juice, onion powder, garlic powder, salt, pepper, and red pepper flakes (if using). Blend until smooth and creamy.
5. **Combine and Bake:**

- Preheat your oven to 375°F (190°C).
- In a large mixing bowl, combine the sautéed vegetables with the blended cashew cream. Mix until well combined.
6. **Transfer to Baking Dish:**
   - Transfer the mixture to an oven-safe baking dish, spreading it out evenly.
7. **Bake:**
   - If using, sprinkle vegan shredded mozzarella or Parmesan cheese on top of the dip.
   - Bake in the preheated oven for 20-25 minutes, or until the dip is heated through and bubbly around the edges.
8. **Serve:**
   - Remove from the oven and let it cool slightly before serving. Garnish with additional red pepper flakes or chopped parsley if desired.
9. **Enjoy:**
   - Serve warm with tortilla chips, crackers, or fresh vegetables for dipping.

Tips:

- **Make Ahead:** You can prepare the dip ahead of time and refrigerate it before baking. When ready to serve, bake as instructed.
- **Storage:** Leftover spinach artichoke dip can be stored in an airtight container in the refrigerator for up to 3-4 days. Reheat in the oven or microwave before serving.
- **Variations:** Feel free to customize the dip by adding vegan cheese alternatives, different herbs, or even a dash of hot sauce for extra flavor.

This vegan spinach artichoke dip is creamy, cheesy, and packed with flavor, making it a crowd-pleasing appetizer that everyone will enjoy, whether they follow a vegan diet or not.

Herb Roasted Acorn Squash

Ingredients:

- 2 medium acorn squash
- 2-3 tablespoons olive oil
- 2-3 cloves garlic, minced
- 1 teaspoon dried thyme (or 1 tablespoon fresh thyme leaves)
- 1 teaspoon dried rosemary (or 1 tablespoon fresh rosemary, chopped)
- 1 teaspoon dried sage (or 1 tablespoon fresh sage leaves, chopped)
- Salt and pepper, to taste

Instructions:

1. **Preheat the Oven:**
   - Preheat your oven to 400°F (200°C).
2. **Prepare the Acorn Squash:**
   - Wash the acorn squash thoroughly. Cut each squash in half vertically and scoop out the seeds and stringy pulp using a spoon. Cut each half into 1-inch thick slices or wedges.
3. **Prepare the Herb Mixture:**
   - In a small bowl, combine olive oil, minced garlic, dried thyme, dried rosemary, dried sage, salt, and pepper. Mix well to combine.
4. **Coat the Squash:**
   - Place the acorn squash slices or wedges in a large mixing bowl. Pour the herb mixture over the squash and toss gently until all pieces are evenly coated with the oil and herbs.
5. **Roast the Squash:**
   - Arrange the coated acorn squash in a single layer on a baking sheet lined with parchment paper or aluminum foil.
6. **Roast in the Oven:**
   - Roast in the preheated oven for 25-30 minutes, or until the squash is tender and caramelized around the edges. Flip the squash halfway through baking to ensure even cooking.
7. **Serve:**
   - Remove from the oven and transfer the herb-roasted acorn squash to a serving platter or dish.
8. **Garnish (optional):**

- Garnish with additional fresh herbs such as chopped parsley or thyme, if desired.
9. **Enjoy:**
   - Serve warm as a delicious side dish or enjoy on its own as a comforting autumn treat.

Tips:

- **Variations:** Feel free to customize the herbs to your liking. You can also add a sprinkle of paprika or a dash of balsamic vinegar for additional flavor.
- **Storage:** Leftover herb-roasted acorn squash can be stored in an airtight container in the refrigerator for up to 3 days. Reheat gently in the oven or microwave before serving.

This herb-roasted acorn squash recipe is simple yet full of flavor, making it a perfect addition to any meal, especially during the fall and winter months. Enjoy the natural sweetness and savory herb blend of this delicious dish!

Vegan Gravy

Ingredients:

- 2 tablespoons olive oil or vegan butter
- 1/4 cup all-purpose flour (or gluten-free flour blend)
- 2 cups vegetable broth
- 1 tablespoon soy sauce or tamari
- 1 teaspoon miso paste (optional, for extra depth of flavor)
- 1/2 teaspoon onion powder
- 1/2 teaspoon garlic powder
- 1/2 teaspoon dried thyme (or 1 teaspoon fresh thyme leaves)
- Salt and pepper, to taste

Instructions:

1. **Prepare the Roux:**
    - In a medium saucepan, heat olive oil or vegan butter over medium heat until melted.
2. **Add Flour:**
    - Sprinkle flour over the melted oil or butter. Whisk continuously to combine and cook for 1-2 minutes, until the mixture turns a light golden brown. This creates a roux, which will thicken the gravy.
3. **Gradually Add Broth:**
    - Slowly pour in vegetable broth, whisking constantly to avoid lumps. Continue whisking until the mixture is smooth and begins to thicken.
4. **Add Flavorings:**
    - Stir in soy sauce or tamari, miso paste (if using), onion powder, garlic powder, and dried thyme. These ingredients add depth and umami to the gravy.
5. **Simmer:**
    - Bring the gravy to a simmer. Reduce heat to low and let it simmer gently for 5-10 minutes, stirring occasionally, until the gravy reaches your desired thickness. If it becomes too thick, you can add more vegetable broth to adjust the consistency.
6. **Season:**
    - Taste the gravy and adjust seasoning with salt and pepper as needed.
7. **Serve:**

- Once the gravy reaches the desired consistency and flavor, remove from heat and serve warm over mashed potatoes, vegan roast, biscuits, or any dish of your choice.

Tips:

- **Variations:** Feel free to customize the gravy by adding fresh herbs like sage or rosemary, or a splash of vegan Worcestershire sauce for additional depth of flavor.
- **Storage:** Leftover vegan gravy can be stored in an airtight container in the refrigerator for up to 4-5 days. Reheat gently on the stovetop or in the microwave, stirring occasionally, until warmed through.
- **Gluten-Free Option:** Use a gluten-free flour blend to make this gravy suitable for those with gluten intolerance or allergies.

This vegan gravy recipe is easy to prepare and pairs wonderfully with a wide range of dishes, making it a staple for any vegan or plant-based meal. Enjoy its rich flavor and creamy texture!

Pear and Arugula Salad

Ingredients:

- 4 cups baby arugula, washed and dried
- 2 ripe pears, thinly sliced
- 1/2 cup walnuts, toasted and roughly chopped
- 1/4 cup dried cranberries or pomegranate arils (optional, for a burst of sweetness)
- 1/4 cup vegan feta cheese, crumbled (optional, for added creaminess and tang)

For the Dressing:

- 3 tablespoons extra virgin olive oil
- 2 tablespoons balsamic vinegar
- 1 tablespoon maple syrup or agave syrup
- 1 teaspoon Dijon mustard
- Salt and pepper, to taste

Instructions:

1. **Prepare the Dressing:**
    - In a small bowl, whisk together olive oil, balsamic vinegar, maple syrup or agave syrup, Dijon mustard, salt, and pepper until well combined. Set aside.
2. **Assemble the Salad:**
    - In a large salad bowl, combine baby arugula, thinly sliced pears, toasted walnuts, and dried cranberries or pomegranate arils (if using). Toss gently to mix.
3. **Add the Dressing:**
    - Drizzle the dressing over the salad ingredients. Start with half of the dressing, toss gently, and add more as needed to coat the salad evenly.
4. **Optional:**
    - If using vegan feta cheese, sprinkle it over the salad just before serving.
5. **Serve:**
    - Transfer the pear and arugula salad to serving plates or a salad bowl. Garnish with additional walnuts or pomegranate arils if desired.

Tips:

- **Variations:** Feel free to add other ingredients such as sliced avocado, cucumber, or a sprinkle of hemp seeds for added texture and nutrition.
- **Make Ahead:** You can prepare the dressing ahead of time and store it in the refrigerator. Toss the salad ingredients with the dressing just before serving to keep the arugula crisp.
- **Presentation:** Serve the pear and arugula salad as a side dish or add grilled tofu or chickpeas to turn it into a satisfying main course.

This pear and arugula salad is a perfect blend of flavors and textures, making it an ideal choice for a light lunch, side dish, or as part of a larger meal. Enjoy the fresh and crisp combination of sweet pears, peppery arugula, and crunchy walnuts!

Glazed Tofu Ham

Ingredients:

- 1 block (14-16 oz) extra-firm tofu
- 1/4 cup soy sauce or tamari
- 2 tablespoons maple syrup or agave syrup
- 1 tablespoon Dijon mustard
- 1 tablespoon olive oil
- 1/2 teaspoon smoked paprika
- 1/2 teaspoon garlic powder
- 1/2 teaspoon onion powder
- 1/4 teaspoon ground black pepper

Glaze:

- 1/4 cup maple syrup
- 1 tablespoon soy sauce or tamari
- 1 tablespoon Dijon mustard
- 1 teaspoon apple cider vinegar
- Pinch of ground cloves (optional)

Instructions:

1. **Prepare the Tofu:**
   - Start by pressing the tofu to remove excess water. Wrap the tofu block in paper towels or a clean kitchen towel. Place it on a plate and place a heavy object on top (such as a cast iron skillet or canned goods). Press for at least 30 minutes.
2. **Marinate the Tofu:**
   - In a shallow dish or container, whisk together soy sauce or tamari, maple syrup or agave syrup, Dijon mustard, olive oil, smoked paprika, garlic powder, onion powder, and black pepper.
   - Once pressed, slice the tofu into thick slices or shapes resembling ham slices.
   - Place the tofu slices into the marinade, ensuring they are well coated. Cover and refrigerate for at least 1 hour, or overnight for best flavor.
3. **Preheat the Oven:**
   - Preheat your oven to 375°F (190°C). Line a baking sheet with parchment paper.

4. **Make the Glaze:**
   - In a small bowl, whisk together maple syrup, soy sauce or tamari, Dijon mustard, apple cider vinegar, and a pinch of ground cloves if using. Set aside.
5. **Bake the Tofu:**
   - Remove the marinated tofu slices from the dish, shaking off any excess marinade. Place them on the prepared baking sheet in a single layer.
   - Brush the tofu slices generously with the prepared glaze, reserving some for basting during baking.
6. **Bake and Glaze:**
   - Bake the tofu ham in the preheated oven for 20-25 minutes, flipping halfway through and brushing with more glaze. Bake until the tofu is caramelized and slightly crispy around the edges.
7. **Serve:**
   - Remove from the oven and let it cool slightly before serving. Serve warm as a main dish or slice it to use in sandwiches or salads.

Tips:

- **Flavor Variations:** You can adjust the marinade and glaze to suit your taste. Add a pinch of ground cloves, ground cinnamon, or even a splash of liquid smoke for a deeper flavor.
- **Storage:** Store leftover glazed tofu ham in an airtight container in the refrigerator for up to 4-5 days. Reheat gently in the oven or microwave before serving.
- **Presentation:** Garnish with fresh herbs like parsley or thyme before serving for a pop of color and added freshness.

This glazed tofu ham recipe provides a delicious alternative for vegans and vegetarians looking to enjoy a festive and flavorful main dish. Enjoy the savory-sweet combination and the hearty texture of this plant-based ham!

Vegan Mac and Cheese

Ingredients:

- 10 oz (about 2 cups) elbow macaroni or any pasta of your choice (use gluten-free pasta if needed)
- 1 cup peeled and diced potatoes (about 1 medium potato)
- 1/2 cup peeled and diced carrots (about 1 medium carrot)
- 1/2 cup raw cashews, soaked in hot water for 1 hour or in cold water overnight
- 1/4 cup nutritional yeast
- 1/4 cup coconut milk or other plant-based milk
- 2 tablespoons olive oil or vegan butter
- 1 tablespoon lemon juice
- 1 teaspoon garlic powder
- 1 teaspoon onion powder
- 1/2 teaspoon smoked paprika
- Salt and pepper, to taste
- Optional: 1/4 teaspoon turmeric (for color)
- Optional: Pinch of cayenne pepper (for heat)

Instructions:

1. **Cook the Pasta:**
   - Cook the elbow macaroni or pasta according to package instructions until al dente. Drain and set aside.
2. **Prepare the Cheese Sauce:**
   - In a medium saucepan, combine diced potatoes and carrots. Cover with water and bring to a boil. Cook for about 10-15 minutes, or until vegetables are tender.
   - Drain the cooked vegetables and transfer them to a blender. Add soaked and drained cashews, nutritional yeast, coconut milk (or other plant-based milk), olive oil or vegan butter, lemon juice, garlic powder, onion powder, smoked paprika, salt, pepper, turmeric (if using), and cayenne pepper (if using).
3. **Blend Until Smooth:**
   - Blend until the mixture is smooth and creamy. You may need to stop and scrape down the sides of the blender a few times to ensure everything is well combined.
4. **Combine Pasta and Sauce:**

- Pour the blended cheese sauce over the cooked pasta in a large pot or mixing bowl. Stir gently to coat the pasta evenly with the sauce.
5. **Heat Through:**
   - Return the pot to low heat and cook, stirring frequently, until the mac and cheese is heated through and the sauce thickens slightly. Adjust the consistency with a splash of plant-based milk if needed.
6. **Serve:**
   - Remove from heat and serve the vegan mac and cheese immediately. Garnish with chopped parsley, smoked paprika, or additional nutritional yeast if desired.

Tips:

- **Variations:** Feel free to customize your vegan mac and cheese by adding sautéed mushrooms, spinach, roasted broccoli, or vegan bacon bits for extra flavor and texture.
- **Storage:** Store leftovers in an airtight container in the refrigerator for up to 3-4 days. Reheat gently on the stovetop or in the microwave, adding a splash of plant-based milk to maintain creaminess.
- **Gluten-Free Option:** Use gluten-free pasta and ensure all ingredients are gluten-free certified.

This vegan mac and cheese recipe is creamy, cheesy, and satisfying, making it a great option for plant-based eaters or anyone looking for a healthier twist on a classic comfort food. Enjoy the creamy goodness without any dairy!

Peppermint Chocolate Bark

Ingredients:

- 12 oz vegan dark chocolate (chopped into small pieces or use chocolate chips)
- 1/2 teaspoon peppermint extract
- 1/2 cup crushed candy canes or peppermint candies

Instructions:

1. **Prepare a Baking Sheet:**
    - Line a baking sheet with parchment paper or a silicone baking mat.
2. **Melt the Chocolate:**
    - In a microwave-safe bowl or using a double boiler, melt the vegan dark chocolate until smooth and completely melted. Stir frequently to prevent burning.
3. **Add Peppermint Extract:**
    - Once melted, stir in the peppermint extract until well combined. Taste and adjust the amount of peppermint extract based on your preference for minty flavor.
4. **Spread Chocolate on Baking Sheet:**
    - Pour the melted chocolate onto the prepared baking sheet. Use a spatula or the back of a spoon to spread it out evenly into a thin layer, about 1/4 to 1/2 inch thick.
5. **Sprinkle with Crushed Peppermint:**
    - Immediately sprinkle the crushed candy canes or peppermint candies evenly over the melted chocolate. Press gently to embed the peppermint pieces into the chocolate.
6. **Set and Harden:**
    - Place the baking sheet in the refrigerator for about 30 minutes to 1 hour, or until the chocolate bark is completely hardened.
7. **Break into Pieces:**
    - Once hardened, remove the chocolate bark from the refrigerator. Use your hands or a knife to break it into pieces of your desired size and shape.
8. **Serve and Enjoy:**
    - Arrange the vegan peppermint chocolate bark pieces on a serving plate or package them in decorative bags or boxes for gifting.

Tips:

- **Storage:** Store the peppermint chocolate bark in an airtight container in a cool place or the refrigerator for up to 2 weeks. Bring to room temperature before serving.
- **Variations:** Experiment with different types of chocolate such as vegan white chocolate or add chopped nuts like almonds or pistachios for added texture and flavor.

This vegan peppermint chocolate bark is a simple yet elegant treat that's perfect for holiday celebrations, gifts, or simply indulging in a sweet, minty snack. Enjoy the combination of smooth chocolate and refreshing peppermint in every bite!

Cinnamon Rolls

Dough Ingredients:

- 1 cup non-dairy milk (such as almond, soy, or oat milk)
- 1/4 cup vegan butter, softened
- 1/4 cup granulated sugar
- 2 1/4 teaspoons (1 packet) active dry yeast
- 3 cups all-purpose flour (plus more for dusting)
- 1/2 teaspoon salt

Filling Ingredients:

- 1/4 cup vegan butter, softened
- 1/2 cup brown sugar, packed
- 1 tablespoon ground cinnamon

Icing Ingredients:

- 1 cup powdered sugar
- 1-2 tablespoons non-dairy milk
- 1/2 teaspoon vanilla extract

Instructions:

1. **Activate Yeast:**
   - Warm the non-dairy milk until it is just warm to the touch (around 110°F or 45°C). Stir in the sugar and sprinkle the yeast on top. Let it sit for 5-10 minutes until foamy.
2. **Make the Dough:**
   - In a large mixing bowl, combine the softened vegan butter, yeast mixture, flour, and salt. Stir until it forms a dough.
   - Knead the dough on a lightly floured surface for about 5-7 minutes, until smooth and elastic.
3. **First Rise:**
   - Place the dough in a greased bowl, cover with a clean kitchen towel, and let it rise in a warm place for about 1-1.5 hours, or until doubled in size.
4. **Prepare the Filling:**
   - In a small bowl, mix together the softened vegan butter, brown sugar, and ground cinnamon until well combined.

5. **Roll out the Dough:**
   - Punch down the risen dough and roll it out on a lightly floured surface into a rectangle, about 1/4 inch thick.
6. **Fill and Roll:**
   - Spread the cinnamon-sugar filling evenly over the rolled-out dough.
   - Starting from one long edge, tightly roll up the dough into a log. Pinch the seam to seal.
7. **Cut into Rolls:**
   - Using a sharp knife or dental floss, cut the dough into 12 even slices.
8. **Second Rise:**
   - Place the cinnamon rolls in a greased baking dish, cover with a kitchen towel, and let them rise for another 30-45 minutes.
9. **Bake:**
   - Preheat the oven to 350°F (175°C).
   - Bake the cinnamon rolls for 20-25 minutes, or until golden brown.
10. **Make the Icing:**
    - While the cinnamon rolls are baking, prepare the icing. In a small bowl, whisk together powdered sugar, non-dairy milk, and vanilla extract until smooth.
11. **Ice and Serve:**
    - Remove the cinnamon rolls from the oven and let them cool for a few minutes. Drizzle the icing over the warm rolls.
    - Serve warm and enjoy!

Tips:

- **Storage:** Cinnamon rolls are best enjoyed fresh on the day they are made. If you have leftovers, store them in an airtight container at room temperature for up to 2 days. Warm them in the microwave before serving.
- **Variations:** Feel free to add chopped nuts or raisins to the filling for extra texture and flavor.

These vegan cinnamon rolls are a delightful treat for breakfast or dessert, with their soft, fluffy texture and sweet cinnamon filling. Enjoy the aroma and taste of freshly baked cinnamon goodness!

Vegan Pumpkin Pie

Ingredients:

For the Pie Crust:

- 1 1/4 cups all-purpose flour
- 1/4 teaspoon salt
- 1/2 cup vegan butter, chilled and cut into small cubes
- 3-4 tablespoons ice water

For the Pumpkin Filling:

- 1 can (15 oz) pumpkin puree (not pumpkin pie filling)
- 3/4 cup full-fat coconut milk (from a can, shaken well before measuring)
- 1/2 cup brown sugar or coconut sugar
- 1/4 cup maple syrup
- 2 tablespoons cornstarch or arrowroot powder
- 1 teaspoon vanilla extract
- 1 1/2 teaspoons ground cinnamon
- 1/2 teaspoon ground ginger
- 1/4 teaspoon ground nutmeg
- 1/4 teaspoon ground cloves
- 1/4 teaspoon salt

Instructions:

For the Pie Crust:

1. **Prepare the Dough:**
    - In a large mixing bowl, whisk together the flour and salt.
    - Add the chilled vegan butter cubes and use a pastry cutter or fork to cut the butter into the flour until the mixture resembles coarse crumbs.
2. **Form the Dough:**
    - Gradually add ice water, 1 tablespoon at a time, mixing with a fork until the dough begins to come together. Be careful not to overmix.
    - Gather the dough into a ball, flatten into a disc, wrap in plastic wrap, and refrigerate for at least 30 minutes.
3. **Roll out the Crust:**
    - Preheat your oven to 375°F (190°C).

- On a lightly floured surface, roll out the chilled dough into a circle about 12 inches in diameter. Carefully transfer the dough to a 9-inch pie dish. Trim and crimp the edges as desired. Prick the bottom of the crust with a fork.

4. **Blind Bake (optional):**
    - For a crispier crust, you can blind bake the crust before adding the filling. Line the pie crust with parchment paper and fill with pie weights or dried beans. Bake in the preheated oven for 15 minutes. Remove the parchment paper and weights and bake for an additional 5 minutes until lightly golden. Set aside to cool.

For the Pumpkin Filling:

1. **Prepare the Filling:**
    - In a large mixing bowl, whisk together the pumpkin puree, coconut milk, brown sugar (or coconut sugar), maple syrup, cornstarch (or arrowroot powder), vanilla extract, cinnamon, ginger, nutmeg, cloves, and salt until smooth and well combined.
2. **Assemble and Bake:**
    - Pour the pumpkin filling into the prepared pie crust, spreading it out evenly.
3. **Bake the Pie:**
    - Bake the pie in the preheated oven for 45-50 minutes, or until the filling is set and the crust is golden brown.
4. **Cool and Serve:**
    - Allow the pie to cool completely on a wire rack before slicing and serving.

Tips:

- **Chilling Time:** Make sure to chill the pie crust dough for at least 30 minutes before rolling it out. This helps prevent shrinkage during baking.
- **Coconut Milk:** Use full-fat coconut milk for a rich and creamy texture in the filling. Shake the can well before measuring to incorporate the cream and liquid.
- **Serve with Toppings:** Serve slices of vegan pumpkin pie with a dollop of coconut whipped cream, a sprinkle of cinnamon, or a drizzle of maple syrup.

This vegan pumpkin pie is a wonderful dessert option for Thanksgiving or any fall gathering, offering the classic flavors of pumpkin and spices in a dairy-free and egg-free recipe. Enjoy the creamy texture and rich taste of this plant-based treat!

Roasted Beet Salad

Ingredients:

- 4 medium-sized beets (red or golden), washed and scrubbed
- 2 tablespoons olive oil
- Salt and pepper, to taste
- 1/2 cup walnuts, toasted and roughly chopped
- 1/4 cup fresh parsley, chopped
- 1/4 cup vegan feta cheese, crumbled (optional)

For the Dressing:

- 3 tablespoons balsamic vinegar
- 2 tablespoons olive oil
- 1 tablespoon maple syrup or agave syrup
- 1 teaspoon Dijon mustard
- Salt and pepper, to taste

Instructions:

1. **Roast the Beets:**
   - Preheat your oven to 400°F (200°C).
   - Trim the tops and roots off the beets. Wrap each beet individually in aluminum foil after drizzling with olive oil, salt, and pepper. Place them on a baking sheet.
   - Roast in the preheated oven for 45-60 minutes, or until the beets are tender when pierced with a fork. Cooking time may vary depending on the size of the beets. Let them cool slightly, then peel off the skins (they should slip off easily) and cut into wedges or cubes.
2. **Toast the Walnuts:**
   - While the beets are roasting, spread the walnuts on a separate baking sheet and toast them in the oven for about 5-7 minutes, until fragrant and lightly golden. Keep an eye on them to prevent burning. Remove and let them cool before chopping roughly.
3. **Prepare the Dressing:**
   - In a small bowl, whisk together balsamic vinegar, olive oil, maple syrup or agave syrup, Dijon mustard, salt, and pepper until well combined. Set aside.
4. **Assemble the Salad:**

- In a large salad bowl, combine the roasted beet wedges or cubes, toasted walnuts, and chopped parsley.
- If using, sprinkle vegan feta cheese over the salad ingredients.
5. **Add Dressing and Toss:**
    - Pour the dressing over the salad and gently toss to coat everything evenly.
6. **Serve:**
    - Transfer the roasted beet salad to a serving platter or individual plates. Serve immediately as a side dish or a light main course.

Tips:

- **Variations:** Add other ingredients like arugula, spinach, or mixed greens for additional freshness and texture.
- **Make-Ahead:** You can roast the beets and toast the walnuts ahead of time. Store them separately in the refrigerator and assemble the salad just before serving.
- **Storage:** Leftover salad can be stored in an airtight container in the refrigerator for up to 2 days. The flavors will meld together even more, making it great for meal prep.

This vegan roasted beet salad is both visually appealing and packed with flavor, making it a perfect choice for a nutritious and satisfying meal or side dish. Enjoy the combination of roasted beets, crunchy walnuts, fresh parsley, and tangy dressing!

Coconut Whipped Cream

Ingredients:

- 1 can (13.5 oz) full-fat coconut milk, chilled in the refrigerator overnight
- 1-2 tablespoons powdered sugar (adjust to taste)
- 1/2 teaspoon vanilla extract

Instructions:

1. **Chill the Coconut Milk:**
   - Place the can of full-fat coconut milk in the refrigerator and leave it overnight, or for at least 8 hours. This allows the coconut cream to separate and solidify at the top of the can.
2. **Prepare the Mixing Bowl:**
   - Before opening the can, place a mixing bowl and beaters (or whisk attachment) in the refrigerator for about 10-15 minutes. This helps to keep everything cold, which is essential for whipping coconut cream.
3. **Open the Coconut Milk:**
   - Open the can of chilled coconut milk without shaking it. Carefully scoop out the solidified coconut cream that has risen to the top and transfer it to the chilled mixing bowl. Reserve any remaining coconut water for other recipes (smoothies, etc.).
4. **Whip the Coconut Cream:**
   - Using a hand mixer or stand mixer fitted with the whisk attachment, beat the coconut cream on medium-high speed for 2-3 minutes, until it becomes fluffy and peaks form.
5. **Sweeten and Flavor:**
   - Add powdered sugar (start with 1 tablespoon and adjust to your desired sweetness) and vanilla extract. Beat for another 1-2 minutes until well combined and smooth.
6. **Serve or Store:**
   - Use the coconut whipped cream immediately as a topping for desserts, fruits, or hot beverages. Alternatively, store any leftovers in an airtight container in the refrigerator for up to 3 days.

Tips:

- **Choosing Coconut Milk:** Use full-fat coconut milk that contains at least 70% coconut extract for the best results in making whipped cream.

- **Consistency:** The consistency of coconut whipped cream can vary depending on the brand of coconut milk used. Some brands may yield a firmer cream than others.
- **Variations:** For flavored coconut whipped cream, you can add cocoa powder for chocolate whipped cream, matcha powder for matcha whipped cream, or other extracts such as almond or peppermint for different flavors.

This vegan coconut whipped cream is creamy, luscious, and dairy-free, making it a versatile topping for various desserts and beverages. Enjoy its rich coconut flavor and light, fluffy texture!

Stuffed Bell Peppers

Ingredients:

- 4 large bell peppers (any color), tops cut off and seeds removed
- 1 cup quinoa, rinsed
- 2 cups vegetable broth or water
- 1 tablespoon olive oil
- 1 small onion, finely chopped
- 2 cloves garlic, minced
- 1 can (15 oz) black beans, drained and rinsed
- 1 cup corn kernels (fresh or frozen)
- 1 teaspoon ground cumin
- 1 teaspoon smoked paprika
- Salt and pepper, to taste
- 1/2 cup tomato sauce or marinara sauce
- 1/2 cup vegan cheese, shredded (optional, for topping)
- Fresh cilantro or parsley, chopped (for garnish)

Instructions:

1. **Preheat the Oven:**
   - Preheat your oven to 375°F (190°C).
2. **Cook Quinoa:**
   - In a medium saucepan, bring the vegetable broth or water to a boil. Add the quinoa, reduce heat to low, cover, and simmer for about 15 minutes, or until the quinoa is cooked and fluffy. Remove from heat and set aside.
3. **Prepare Bell Peppers:**
   - Cut the tops off the bell peppers and remove the seeds and membranes. If the peppers do not stand upright, you can slice a thin layer off the bottom to stabilize them.
4. **Prepare the Filling:**
   - In a large skillet, heat olive oil over medium heat. Add chopped onion and cook until softened, about 5 minutes. Add minced garlic and cook for another 1-2 minutes until fragrant.
   - Stir in black beans, corn kernels, ground cumin, smoked paprika, salt, and pepper. Cook for 3-4 minutes, stirring occasionally, until heated through and well combined.
5. **Combine Quinoa and Filling:**

- Add the cooked quinoa to the skillet with the bean and corn mixture. Stir in tomato sauce or marinara sauce. Mix well to combine and cook for another 2-3 minutes, allowing the flavors to meld together. Adjust seasoning to taste.
6. **Stuff the Bell Peppers:**
    - Arrange the hollowed-out bell peppers in a baking dish. Spoon the quinoa and bean mixture evenly into each pepper until filled.
7. **Bake:**
    - Cover the baking dish with foil and bake in the preheated oven for 30-35 minutes, or until the bell peppers are tender and slightly charred.
8. **Add Vegan Cheese (Optional):**
    - If using vegan cheese, remove the foil from the baking dish and sprinkle shredded vegan cheese over the stuffed bell peppers. Return to the oven for another 5-7 minutes, or until the cheese is melted and bubbly.
9. **Serve:**
    - Remove from the oven and let the stuffed bell peppers cool for a few minutes before serving. Garnish with fresh chopped cilantro or parsley if desired.

Tips:

- **Variations:** Feel free to customize the filling with other vegetables such as diced tomatoes, spinach, or zucchini. You can also add cooked lentils or chickpeas for extra protein.
- **Make-Ahead:** Prepare the filling and stuff the bell peppers ahead of time. Cover tightly with foil or plastic wrap and refrigerate until ready to bake.
- **Storage:** Leftover stuffed bell peppers can be stored in an airtight container in the refrigerator for up to 3 days. Reheat in the oven or microwave before serving.

These vegan stuffed bell peppers are wholesome, filling, and packed with nutritious ingredients. They make a satisfying main dish that's perfect for any meal, whether for a weeknight dinner or a special occasion. Enjoy the blend of flavors and textures in every bite!

Vegan Yorkshire Pudding

Ingredients:

- 1 cup all-purpose flour
- 1 cup non-dairy milk (such as almond, soy, or oat milk)
- 1/2 cup water
- 1/2 teaspoon salt
- 1/2 teaspoon baking powder
- 3 tablespoons vegetable oil or melted vegan butter

Instructions:

1. **Preheat Oven:**
   - Preheat your oven to 425°F (220°C). Place a muffin tin or Yorkshire pudding tin in the oven to heat up.
2. **Prepare Batter:**
   - In a mixing bowl, whisk together the flour, non-dairy milk, water, salt, and baking powder until smooth and well combined. The batter should be thin, similar to pancake batter consistency.
3. **Rest the Batter:**
   - Let the batter rest for at least 15-20 minutes. This allows the flour to hydrate and helps achieve a lighter texture.
4. **Heat Oil:**
   - Add 1/2 to 1 teaspoon of vegetable oil or melted vegan butter into each section of the hot muffin tin or Yorkshire pudding tin. Place it back into the oven for a couple of minutes until the oil is very hot and just starting to smoke.
5. **Pour Batter:**
   - Carefully remove the hot tin from the oven and quickly pour the batter into each section, filling them about halfway.
6. **Bake:**
   - Place the tin back into the oven and bake for 20-25 minutes, or until the Yorkshire puddings are puffed up and golden brown.
7. **Serve:**
   - Remove from the oven and serve immediately while hot. Vegan Yorkshire puddings are traditionally served with gravy.

Tips:

- **Hot Tin:** It's crucial that the tin and oil are very hot before pouring in the batter. This helps create the signature puffiness of Yorkshire puddings.
- **Non-Dairy Milk:** Use unsweetened non-dairy milk for the batter to avoid adding sweetness to the puddings.
- **Gravy:** Vegan gravy made from vegetable broth and thickened with flour or cornstarch complements Yorkshire puddings perfectly.

These vegan Yorkshire puddings are a great addition to a holiday meal or Sunday roast, providing a comforting and satisfying accompaniment. Enjoy their light and fluffy texture, perfect for soaking up savory sauces!

Holiday Spice Cake

Ingredients:

- 2 cups all-purpose flour
- 1 teaspoon baking powder
- 1/2 teaspoon baking soda
- 1/2 teaspoon salt
- 1 teaspoon ground cinnamon
- 1/2 teaspoon ground nutmeg
- 1/2 teaspoon ground cloves
- 1/2 teaspoon ground ginger
- 1 cup unsweetened applesauce
- 1 cup granulated sugar or coconut sugar
- 1/2 cup vegetable oil
- 1/2 cup non-dairy milk (such as almond, soy, or oat milk)
- 1 teaspoon vanilla extract
- 1 tablespoon apple cider vinegar

Optional Additions:

- 1/2 cup chopped nuts (such as walnuts or pecans)
- 1/2 cup raisins or chopped dried fruit
- Vegan cream cheese frosting or powdered sugar (for topping)

Instructions:

1. **Preheat Oven and Prepare Pan:**
   - Preheat your oven to 350°F (175°C). Grease and flour a 9-inch round cake pan or line it with parchment paper.
2. **Mix Dry Ingredients:**
   - In a medium bowl, whisk together the flour, baking powder, baking soda, salt, cinnamon, nutmeg, cloves, and ginger until well combined. Set aside.
3. **Prepare Wet Ingredients:**
   - In a large mixing bowl, combine the applesauce, sugar, vegetable oil, non-dairy milk, vanilla extract, and apple cider vinegar. Mix until smooth and well incorporated.
4. **Combine and Mix:**
   - Gradually add the dry ingredients to the wet ingredients, mixing until just combined. Be careful not to overmix.

        - If using, fold in chopped nuts and raisins or dried fruit at this stage.
5. **Bake:**
    - Pour the batter into the prepared cake pan and smooth the top with a spatula.
    - Bake in the preheated oven for 30-35 minutes, or until a toothpick inserted into the center of the cake comes out clean.
6. **Cool:**
    - Remove the cake from the oven and let it cool in the pan for 10 minutes. Then, transfer it to a wire rack to cool completely.
7. **Serve:**
    - Once cooled, dust the top with powdered sugar or frost with vegan cream cheese frosting if desired.
    - Slice and serve the vegan holiday spice cake. Enjoy with a cup of tea or coffee!

Tips:

- **Variations:** Feel free to adjust the spices to your preference. You can also add grated carrots or zucchini for a twist on traditional spice cake.
- **Storage:** Store leftovers in an airtight container at room temperature for up to 3 days, or in the refrigerator for up to 5 days. Bring to room temperature or gently reheat before serving.
- **Frosting:** If opting for frosting, consider a vegan cream cheese frosting flavored with cinnamon or vanilla to complement the spice flavors of the cake.

This vegan holiday spice cake is moist, aromatic, and full of festive flavors, making it a wonderful treat for celebrations or as a cozy dessert during the holiday season. Enjoy the warmth of cinnamon, nutmeg, cloves, and ginger in every bite!

Quinoa Stuffed Acorn Squash

Ingredients:

- 2 acorn squash, halved and seeds removed
- 1 cup quinoa, rinsed
- 2 cups vegetable broth or water
- 1 tablespoon olive oil
- 1 small onion, finely chopped
- 2 cloves garlic, minced
- 1 bell pepper, diced (any color)
- 1 small zucchini, diced
- 1 carrot, diced
- 1/2 cup corn kernels (fresh or frozen)
- 1 teaspoon ground cumin
- 1 teaspoon smoked paprika
- Salt and pepper, to taste
- 1/4 cup chopped fresh parsley or cilantro
- Optional: 1/4 cup chopped nuts (such as walnuts or pecans)
- Optional: Vegan cheese (such as shredded vegan mozzarella or nutritional yeast for topping)

Instructions:

1. **Preheat Oven:**
    - Preheat your oven to 400°F (200°C).
2. **Prepare Acorn Squash:**
    - Cut the acorn squash in half lengthwise and scoop out the seeds. Place the squash halves cut side down on a baking sheet lined with parchment paper. Bake for 30-35 minutes, or until the squash is tender when pierced with a fork.
3. **Cook Quinoa:**
    - While the squash is baking, rinse the quinoa under cold water. In a medium saucepan, bring the vegetable broth or water to a boil. Add the quinoa, reduce heat to low, cover, and simmer for about 15 minutes, or until the quinoa is cooked and liquid is absorbed. Remove from heat and fluff with a fork.
4. **Prepare the Filling:**

- In a large skillet, heat olive oil over medium heat. Add chopped onion and cook until softened, about 5 minutes. Add minced garlic and cook for another minute until fragrant.
- Add diced bell pepper, zucchini, carrot, and corn kernels to the skillet. Cook for 5-7 minutes, stirring occasionally, until the vegetables are tender.
- Stir in ground cumin, smoked paprika, salt, and pepper. Cook for another 1-2 minutes to toast the spices.

5. **Combine Quinoa and Vegetables:**
    - Add the cooked quinoa to the skillet with the vegetables. Mix well to combine. Taste and adjust seasoning if needed. Stir in chopped fresh parsley or cilantro. If using, add chopped nuts for extra texture.

6. **Assemble and Serve:**
    - Once the acorn squash halves are baked and tender, flip them over so they are cut side up. Fill each squash half with the quinoa and vegetable mixture.
    - If desired, sprinkle with vegan cheese or nutritional yeast for added flavor.

7. **Bake Again (Optional):**
    - Place the stuffed acorn squash back in the oven for another 10-15 minutes to heat through and melt the cheese, if using.

8. **Serve:**
    - Remove from the oven and let cool slightly before serving. Garnish with additional fresh herbs if desired.

Tips:

- **Variations:** Feel free to customize the filling with your favorite vegetables and herbs. You can also add cooked beans or lentils for extra protein.
- **Make-Ahead:** Prepare the quinoa and vegetable filling ahead of time. Store in an airtight container in the refrigerator for up to 2 days. When ready to serve, reheat the filling and stuff the acorn squash halves.
- **Presentation:** Serve the stuffed acorn squash halves on a bed of greens or alongside a fresh salad for a complete meal.

This quinoa stuffed acorn squash is wholesome, filling, and packed with flavor and nutrients. It's a great option for a vegan dinner or holiday meal, offering a beautiful presentation and satisfying taste!

Vegan Gingersnaps

Ingredients:

- 2 cups all-purpose flour
- 1 teaspoon baking soda
- 1/2 teaspoon salt
- 1 teaspoon ground ginger
- 1 teaspoon ground cinnamon
- 1/2 teaspoon ground cloves
- 1/2 teaspoon ground nutmeg
- 1/2 cup vegan butter, softened (such as Earth Balance)
- 1/2 cup brown sugar, packed
- 1/4 cup molasses
- 1 teaspoon vanilla extract
- Granulated sugar, for rolling

Instructions:

1. **Preheat Oven:**
   - Preheat your oven to 350°F (175°C). Line baking sheets with parchment paper or silicone baking mats.
2. **Mix Dry Ingredients:**
   - In a medium bowl, whisk together the flour, baking soda, salt, ground ginger, cinnamon, cloves, and nutmeg until well combined. Set aside.
3. **Cream Wet Ingredients:**
   - In a large bowl or the bowl of a stand mixer, beat together the softened vegan butter and brown sugar until creamy and smooth, about 2-3 minutes.
4. **Add Molasses and Vanilla:**
   - Add the molasses and vanilla extract to the butter-sugar mixture. Beat until well combined.
5. **Combine Dry and Wet Ingredients:**
   - Gradually add the dry ingredients to the wet ingredients, mixing on low speed until a thick dough forms. Scrape down the sides of the bowl as needed.
6. **Chill the Dough (Optional):**

- For easier handling, you can chill the dough in the refrigerator for 30 minutes to 1 hour. This step helps to firm up the dough and prevents spreading during baking.
7. **Shape Cookies:**
    - Scoop tablespoon-sized portions of dough and roll them into balls. Roll each ball in granulated sugar until coated.
8. **Bake:**
    - Place the coated dough balls on the prepared baking sheets, spacing them about 2 inches apart. Flatten each ball slightly with the palm of your hand.
    - Bake in the preheated oven for 10-12 minutes, or until the cookies are set and lightly golden around the edges.
9. **Cool and Serve:**
    - Allow the cookies to cool on the baking sheets for 5 minutes before transferring them to a wire rack to cool completely.
10. **Store:**
    - Once cooled, store the vegan gingersnaps in an airtight container at room temperature for up to 1 week. They also freeze well for longer storage.

Tips:

- **Molasses Substitution:** If you prefer a milder flavor, you can use light molasses instead of dark molasses.
- **Spice Level:** Adjust the amount of ground spices according to your taste preferences. You can increase the ginger for a spicier kick.
- **Texture:** For softer cookies, bake for less time; for crunchier cookies, bake for a few minutes longer.

These vegan gingersnaps are a delightful treat with a perfect balance of spices and sweetness. Enjoy them with a cup of tea or coffee during the holidays or anytime you crave a tasty cookie!

Cranberry Walnut Bread

Ingredients:

- 1 1/2 cups all-purpose flour
- 1/2 cup whole wheat flour
- 1 teaspoon baking powder
- 1/2 teaspoon baking soda
- 1/2 teaspoon salt
- 1/2 cup brown sugar or coconut sugar
- 1/4 cup maple syrup or agave syrup
- 1/4 cup melted coconut oil or vegetable oil
- 1 cup non-dairy milk (such as almond, soy, or oat milk)
- 1 teaspoon vanilla extract
- 1 cup fresh or frozen cranberries, coarsely chopped
- 1/2 cup walnuts, chopped

Instructions:

1. **Preheat Oven:**
    - Preheat your oven to 350°F (175°C). Grease a 9x5-inch loaf pan or line it with parchment paper.
2. **Mix Dry Ingredients:**
    - In a large bowl, whisk together the all-purpose flour, whole wheat flour, baking powder, baking soda, and salt.
3. **Prepare Wet Ingredients:**
    - In another bowl, mix together the brown sugar (or coconut sugar), maple syrup (or agave syrup), melted coconut oil (or vegetable oil), non-dairy milk, and vanilla extract until well combined.
4. **Combine Wet and Dry Ingredients:**
    - Pour the wet ingredients into the bowl of dry ingredients. Stir gently until just combined. Do not overmix.
5. **Add Cranberries and Walnuts:**
    - Gently fold in the chopped cranberries and walnuts into the batter.
6. **Bake:**
    - Pour the batter into the prepared loaf pan and spread evenly. Smooth the top with a spatula.
    - Bake in the preheated oven for 50-60 minutes, or until a toothpick inserted into the center comes out clean.

7. **Cool:**
   - Allow the bread to cool in the pan for 10 minutes, then remove it from the pan and transfer it to a wire rack to cool completely.
8. **Slice and Serve:**
   - Once cooled, slice the cranberry walnut bread and serve. Enjoy it warm or at room temperature.

Tips:

- **Storage:** Store leftovers in an airtight container at room temperature for up to 3 days, or in the refrigerator for longer freshness.
- **Variations:** You can add a teaspoon of orange zest for a citrusy twist, or replace walnuts with pecans or almonds for variation.
- **Make-Ahead:** This bread freezes well. Wrap slices or the entire loaf tightly in plastic wrap and store in a freezer-safe container for up to 1 month. Thaw slices at room temperature or in a toaster oven when ready to eat.

This vegan cranberry walnut bread is moist, flavorful, and packed with wholesome ingredients. It's perfect for breakfast, a snack, or as a delightful addition to any holiday spread. Enjoy the combination of tart cranberries, crunchy walnuts, and warm spices in every slice!

Vegan Biscuits with Mushroom Gravy

Vegan Biscuits Ingredients:

- 2 cups all-purpose flour
- 1 tablespoon baking powder
- 1/2 teaspoon baking soda
- 1/2 teaspoon salt
- 1/2 cup vegan butter or margarine, chilled and cut into small cubes
- 3/4 cup non-dairy milk (such as almond, soy, or oat milk)
- 1 tablespoon apple cider vinegar

Mushroom Gravy Ingredients:

- 2 tablespoons olive oil
- 1 onion, finely chopped
- 2 cloves garlic, minced
- 8 oz mushrooms (cremini or button), sliced
- 1/4 cup all-purpose flour
- 2 cups vegetable broth
- 1/2 cup non-dairy milk (such as almond, soy, or oat milk)
- 1 tablespoon soy sauce or tamari
- 1/2 teaspoon dried thyme
- Salt and pepper, to taste

Instructions:

Vegan Biscuits:

1. **Preheat Oven:**
    - Preheat your oven to 425°F (220°C). Line a baking sheet with parchment paper.
2. **Mix Dry Ingredients:**
    - In a large bowl, whisk together the all-purpose flour, baking powder, baking soda, and salt.
3. **Cut in Vegan Butter:**
    - Add the chilled vegan butter cubes to the flour mixture. Use a pastry cutter or fork to cut the butter into the flour until it resembles coarse crumbs.
4. **Combine Wet Ingredients:**

- In a measuring cup, combine the non-dairy milk and apple cider vinegar. Let it sit for a few minutes to curdle slightly.
5. **Form Dough:**
    - Pour the non-dairy milk mixture into the flour mixture. Stir gently until just combined and a dough forms. Be careful not to overmix.
6. **Shape Biscuits:**
    - Transfer the dough onto a lightly floured surface. Pat the dough into a rectangle about 1-inch thick. Use a biscuit cutter or a drinking glass to cut out biscuits. Place them on the prepared baking sheet, spacing them about 1 inch apart.
7. **Bake:**
    - Bake in the preheated oven for 12-15 minutes, or until the biscuits are golden brown on top.
8. **Cool:**
    - Remove the biscuits from the oven and let them cool slightly on a wire rack.

Mushroom Gravy:

1. **Sauté Onions and Garlic:**
    - In a large skillet, heat olive oil over medium heat. Add the chopped onion and sauté until translucent, about 5 minutes. Add minced garlic and cook for another minute until fragrant.
2. **Add Mushrooms:**
    - Add sliced mushrooms to the skillet. Cook for 5-7 minutes, stirring occasionally, until the mushrooms are tender and golden brown.
3. **Make Roux:**
    - Sprinkle flour over the mushrooms and stir to coat evenly. Cook for 1-2 minutes, stirring constantly, to cook off the raw flour taste.
4. **Add Liquid:**
    - Gradually pour in the vegetable broth and non-dairy milk, stirring constantly to prevent lumps. Bring the mixture to a simmer, stirring occasionally.
5. **Season and Simmer:**
    - Stir in soy sauce (or tamari), dried thyme, salt, and pepper. Reduce heat to low and simmer for 5-7 minutes, or until the gravy has thickened to your desired consistency. Taste and adjust seasoning if needed.
6. **Serve:**

- Split the warm biscuits in half and ladle mushroom gravy over each biscuit. Serve immediately.

Tips:

- **Biscuit Tips:** Handle the biscuit dough gently and avoid overworking it to ensure tender biscuits.
- **Gravy Variations:** Feel free to add chopped herbs like parsley or sage to the gravy for extra flavor.
- **Make-Ahead:** Both the biscuits and gravy can be prepared ahead of time. Store biscuits in an airtight container at room temperature and reheat before serving. Reheat gravy gently on the stovetop, adding a splash of water or broth to thin it out if needed.

Enjoy these vegan biscuits with mushroom gravy as a comforting and satisfying meal, perfect for breakfast or brunch gatherings!

Chocolate Peppermint Cupcakes

Ingredients:

For the Cupcakes:

- 1 cup non-dairy milk (such as almond, soy, or oat milk)
- 1 teaspoon apple cider vinegar
- 3/4 cup granulated sugar
- 1/3 cup melted coconut oil or vegetable oil
- 1 teaspoon vanilla extract
- 1 cup all-purpose flour
- 1/3 cup cocoa powder
- 3/4 teaspoon baking soda
- 1/2 teaspoon baking powder
- 1/4 teaspoon salt

For the Peppermint Buttercream Frosting:

- 1/2 cup vegan butter, softened (such as Earth Balance)
- 2 cups powdered sugar
- 1/2 teaspoon peppermint extract
- 1-2 tablespoons non-dairy milk
- Vegan chocolate chips or crushed candy canes, for garnish (optional)

Instructions:

For the Cupcakes:

1. **Preheat Oven:**
    - Preheat your oven to 350°F (175°C). Line a muffin tin with cupcake liners.
2. **Prepare Wet Ingredients:**
    - In a small bowl or measuring cup, combine the non-dairy milk and apple cider vinegar. Let it sit for a few minutes to curdle and create vegan buttermilk.
3. **Mix Wet Ingredients:**
    - In a large mixing bowl, whisk together the granulated sugar, melted coconut oil (or vegetable oil), and vanilla extract until well combined.
4. **Combine Dry Ingredients:**
    - In another bowl, sift together the all-purpose flour, cocoa powder, baking soda, baking powder, and salt.

5. **Make Batter:**
    - Add the vegan buttermilk mixture to the wet ingredients and stir until smooth. Gradually add the dry ingredients to the wet ingredients, mixing until just combined. Be careful not to overmix.
6. **Fill Cupcake Liners:**
    - Spoon the batter into the prepared cupcake liners, filling each about 2/3 full.
7. **Bake:**
    - Bake in the preheated oven for 18-20 minutes, or until a toothpick inserted into the center of a cupcake comes out clean.
8. **Cool:**
    - Remove the cupcakes from the oven and let them cool in the muffin tin for 5 minutes. Then transfer them to a wire rack to cool completely before frosting.

For the Peppermint Buttercream Frosting:

1. **Cream Vegan Butter:**
    - In a large mixing bowl, beat the softened vegan butter with an electric mixer until creamy.
2. **Add Sugar and Peppermint Extract:**
    - Gradually add the powdered sugar, about 1/2 cup at a time, beating well after each addition. Add the peppermint extract and continue beating until light and fluffy.
3. **Adjust Consistency:**
    - If the frosting is too thick, add 1-2 tablespoons of non-dairy milk, a little at a time, until desired consistency is reached.
4. **Frost Cupcakes:**
    - Once the cupcakes are completely cool, frost them with the peppermint buttercream frosting using a piping bag or offset spatula.
5. **Garnish (Optional):**
    - Sprinkle vegan chocolate chips or crushed candy canes on top of the frosted cupcakes for decoration.
6. **Serve:**
    - Serve these delicious vegan chocolate peppermint cupcakes immediately, or store them in an airtight container in the refrigerator until ready to serve.

Tips:

- **Variations:** For an extra chocolatey flavor, you can add vegan chocolate chips to the cupcake batter before baking.
- **Storage:** Store leftover cupcakes in an airtight container in the refrigerator for up to 3 days.
- **Make-Ahead:** You can bake the cupcakes and prepare the frosting ahead of time. Frost the cupcakes just before serving for the best presentation.

These vegan chocolate peppermint cupcakes are moist, chocolatey, and topped with a refreshing peppermint buttercream frosting. They are sure to be a hit at any holiday gathering or special occasion! Enjoy the festive flavors in every bite.

Apple Cranberry Crisp

Ingredients:

For the Filling:

- 4 cups apples, peeled, cored, and sliced (about 4-5 medium apples, such as Granny Smith or Honeycrisp)
- 1 cup fresh or frozen cranberries
- 1/4 cup granulated sugar
- 1 tablespoon cornstarch or arrowroot powder
- 1 tablespoon lemon juice
- 1/2 teaspoon ground cinnamon
- 1/4 teaspoon ground nutmeg
- 1/4 teaspoon ground ginger

For the Crisp Topping:

- 1 cup old-fashioned rolled oats (gluten-free if needed)
- 1/2 cup all-purpose flour (or almond flour for gluten-free)
- 1/2 cup packed brown sugar or coconut sugar
- 1/2 teaspoon ground cinnamon
- 1/4 teaspoon salt
- 1/2 cup vegan butter or coconut oil, melted

Instructions:

1. **Preheat Oven:**
    - Preheat your oven to 350°F (175°C). Lightly grease a 9x9-inch baking dish or similar size.
2. **Prepare Filling:**
    - In a large bowl, combine the sliced apples, cranberries, granulated sugar, cornstarch (or arrowroot powder), lemon juice, cinnamon, nutmeg, and ginger. Toss until the fruit is evenly coated.
3. **Transfer to Baking Dish:**
    - Transfer the apple cranberry mixture to the prepared baking dish, spreading it out evenly.
4. **Make Crisp Topping:**
    - In another bowl, combine the rolled oats, all-purpose flour (or almond flour), brown sugar (or coconut sugar), cinnamon, and salt. Mix well.

5. **Add Melted Butter:**
   - Pour the melted vegan butter (or coconut oil) over the oat mixture. Stir until well combined and the mixture resembles coarse crumbs.
6. **Top the Fruit Mixture:**
   - Sprinkle the crisp topping evenly over the apple cranberry mixture in the baking dish, covering it completely.
7. **Bake:**
   - Bake in the preheated oven for 35-40 minutes, or until the fruit is bubbling and the topping is golden brown.
8. **Cool and Serve:**
   - Remove from the oven and let it cool for 10-15 minutes before serving. Serve warm with vegan ice cream or whipped coconut cream, if desired.

Tips:

- **Variations:** Feel free to add chopped nuts (such as pecans or walnuts) to the crisp topping for extra crunch and flavor.
- **Storage:** Store any leftovers in an airtight container in the refrigerator for up to 3 days. Reheat in the oven or microwave before serving.
- **Make-Ahead:** You can prepare the apple cranberry filling and crisp topping ahead of time. Store them separately in the refrigerator until ready to assemble and bake.

This vegan apple cranberry crisp is a delightful combination of sweet and tart flavors, topped with a crunchy oat topping. It's perfect for a cozy dessert on a chilly evening or as a treat for holiday gatherings. Enjoy the comforting warmth of baked apples and cranberries in every spoonful!

Spiced Hot Chocolate

Ingredients:

- 2 cups non-dairy milk (such as almond, soy, or oat milk)
- 2 tablespoons cocoa powder (unsweetened)
- 2-3 tablespoons maple syrup or agave syrup (adjust to taste)
- 1/2 teaspoon ground cinnamon
- 1/4 teaspoon ground nutmeg
- 1/4 teaspoon ground ginger
- 1/8 teaspoon ground cloves
- Pinch of salt
- 1 teaspoon vanilla extract
- Vegan whipped cream or coconut whipped cream, for topping (optional)
- Ground cinnamon or cocoa powder, for dusting (optional)

Instructions:

1. **Heat Milk:**
   - In a small saucepan, heat the non-dairy milk over medium heat until it starts to simmer. Stir occasionally to prevent scalding.
2. **Mix Cocoa Powder and Spices:**
   - In a small bowl, whisk together the cocoa powder, ground cinnamon, ground nutmeg, ground ginger, ground cloves, and pinch of salt.
3. **Combine Ingredients:**
   - Once the milk is simmering, reduce the heat to low. Whisk in the cocoa powder mixture and maple syrup (or agave syrup) until smooth and well combined.
4. **Simmer:**
   - Let the hot chocolate simmer gently for 2-3 minutes, stirring occasionally, to allow the flavors to meld together.
5. **Add Vanilla Extract:**
   - Remove the saucepan from the heat and stir in the vanilla extract.
6. **Serve:**
   - Pour the spiced hot chocolate into mugs. Top with vegan whipped cream or coconut whipped cream if desired.
7. **Garnish (Optional):**
   - Sprinkle with a dusting of ground cinnamon or cocoa powder for extra flavor and presentation.

8. **Enjoy:**
    - Serve immediately and enjoy the comforting warmth of spiced hot chocolate!

Tips:

- **Adjust Sweetness:** Taste the hot chocolate before serving and adjust the amount of maple syrup or agave syrup to suit your preference for sweetness.
- **Variations:** You can customize your spiced hot chocolate by adding a pinch of cayenne pepper for a spicy kick, or substituting some of the spices with your favorites like cardamom or allspice.
- **Make-Ahead:** Prepare the hot chocolate base ahead of time and reheat gently on the stove or in the microwave before serving. Stir well before pouring into mugs.

This vegan spiced hot chocolate is a delightful treat that combines rich cocoa with warming spices, perfect for cozy evenings or holiday gatherings. Enjoy its comforting flavors and soothing warmth!

www.ingramcontent.com/pod-product-compliance
Lightning Source LLC
LaVergne TN
LVHW081557060526
838201LV00054B/1936